THE SUN

<u>All About</u>

Correcting Past Skin Damages, Proven Methods For Sun Protection, Vitamin D Deficiency And Some Fun With The Sun

By Ori Laor

Disclaimer

The methods described in this eBook are the author's thoughts. They are not intended to be a definitive set of instructions for this project. You may discover there are other methods and materials to accomplish the same result.

This book is not intended to be a substitute for the medical advice of a licensed physician. The reader should consult with their doctor in any matters relating to his/her health.

The information contained within this eBook is strictly for educational purposes. If you wish to apply ideas contained in this eBook, you are taking full responsibility for your actions.

The author has made every effort to ensure the accuracy of the information within this book was correct at time of publication. The author does not assume and at this moment disclaims any liability to any party for any loss, damage, or disruption caused by errors or omissions, whether such errors or omissions result from accident, negligence, or any other cause.

Thank you very much
Ori Laor

Table of Contents

Personal Introduction

Thank you for downloading this fantastic guide - "The Sun – All About - Correcting Past Skin Damages, Proven Methods For Sun Protection, Vitamin D Deficiency And Some Fun With The Sun". I have lived in Israel, a desert Climate, all my life so I have a very long history with the sun. Sun is fun but it can also leed to dameges in the skin and even cancer. So I wrote this book in order to establish good relationship with the sun.

The sun is the source of life, Every animal and plant needs the sun. This book is about the good energies of the sun, how to enjoy the sun and how to keep the best protection from the sun dangers and correct the damages.

As children, we were taught during science classes that if there was no sun there would have been no life at all on our planet. All forms of life depend on the solar energy. In the absence of this energy-giving life, the earth would be deprived from all forms of life.

Ultraviolet rays are responsible for chemical reaction on human body, when sufficient amount of it comes into contact with the human skin it produces vitamin D. This vitamin helps in growth of humans and protects children from racket disease. However, overexposure to the sun will cause not only sunburn and pigmentation but also skin cancer. The sun, which is the source of solar energy, is a huge ball of fire which remains stationary.

Solar is a Latin word which mean sun. There is great deal of matter in the sun. Nuclear reaction inside the sun takes place continuously and non-stop. So they make the sun a vibrant source of energy which is emitted in all directions. Some of the vast energy reaches the earth. The energy from the sun that is received by the earth is minimal and yet it is enough to sustain life.

The actual skin color of different humans is affected by many components, although the single most important component is the pigment melanin. Melanin is produced within the skin in cells called melanocytes and it is the main determine of the skin color of darker-skinned humans. The skin color of people with light skin is determined mainly by the bluish-white connective tissue under the dermis and by the hemoglobin circulating in the veins of the dermis.

The Color of our Body is not entirely uniform; for example, the skin of the palm of the hand and the sole of the feet is lighter than most other skin in the body, and this is especially noticeable in darker-skinned people. Many people have pigmentation spots or other colored spots on the fave or other body parts.

Since the down of history keeping the skin white and smooth was kept almost sacred, the nobility in all centuries never exposed their skin to the sun, using special creams and umbrellas and in many countries even today white skin especially in the face is considered a sign of beauty and wealth. In Africa women used to rub there skin with mud as a measure of protection against the sun.

As a professional Aestetician, I read and experiment and I have tried to create a fun ebook that will help you understand the powerfull energies of the sun the good and the bad. I hope it helps.

For my new Kindle readers, I offer a Free Voucher Gift of 20$. You can find a keyword at the end of this book. Please send it to my mail orilaor@outlook.com, and you will receive a discount for any porches you make for yourself, a

member of your family or a friend in LAOR website www.laorcare.com**.**

About Me

I have a passion for Beauty, Skincare, Anti-aging and well-being methods. In my extensive exploration around the world, I gathered sacred pieces of information that helped me and then other people from all walks of life to look and feel younger. I hold a BA in Art and diplomas for Makeup Artist, Para Medical Aesthetician, Aromatherapy, Naturopathy, and Nutrition consultant. I am a well-known name in T.V scene and in the cosmetic industry, including treating many celebrities. When I was 30 years old, I quit working for others and founded LAOR, a House of natural Beauty and Professional Skin Care and treatments for the face, Body, and Mind.

Since an early age, I suffered from my skin and was carried away with Skincare research, science and well-being. I worked in beauty and style departments in New York and Tel Aviv, based on my experience I invented a revolutionary practice for treating the skin from within – **The Layer system,**

Complied with a line of professional cosmetic products and treatments for the face to treat any skin problem.

I entered the natural cosmetics world with a unique world-view and with one simple, honest purpose: to create a different kind of cosmetic that is Natural and effective. My desire is that each product would provide each with the essence of beauty, based on effective ingredients.

Now, for the past Two Decades, I am designing the products that Men and women across the world love, helping them to look and feel younger with all the secrets of skin care. When I am not working, I love to design and create, read, write and paint. My quest is to bring more beauty to the world and raise self-awareness.

Let's Get Started!

<u>Chapter 1</u>

The Sun

All About

The Sun is the star at the center of the Solar System. It is a nearly perfect sphere of hot plasma, with internal convective motion that generates a magnetic field via a dynamo process. It is by far the most important source of energy for life on Earth.

Let's consider that there may be two billion parts or strength of energy in the sun. A billion is equal to one thousand million or a hundred crore. Out of this huge energy of two billions, the earth's surface receive only one small part.

Its diameter of the sun is about 109 times of Earth, and its mass is about 330,000 times of Earth, accounting for about 99.86% of the total mass of the Solar System. About three-quarters of the Sun's mass consists of hydrogen (~73%); the rest is mostly helium (~25%), with much smaller quantities of heavier elements, including oxygen, carbon, neon, and iron.

The first condition of the sun is that **it must have a mass falling within a certain range.** Though debated, this range is generally accepted to be between approximately 1.4 x 1029 kg and 3.0 x 1032 kg. (This range is often describe as at least 75 times the mass of Jupiter and no more than 150 times the mass of the Sun itself.) The second and most important condition is that **nuclear fusion must be present.** Nuclear fusion is the process whereby two lighter atomic nuclei join or "fuse" together to produce a heavier atomic nucleus. In the context of stars, hydrogen is the lighter and helium the heavier.

The Size Of The Sun

The sun is the largest and the most massive object in the solar system, but it is just a medium-sized star among the hundreds of billions of stars in the Milky Way galaxy.

Radius, Diameter & Perimeter

The sun is nearly a perfect sphere. Its equatorial diameter and its polar diameter differ by only 6.2 miles (10 km). The mean radius of the sun is 432,450 miles (696,000 kilometers), which makes its diameter about 864,938 miles (1.392 million km).

You could line up 109 Earths across the face of the sun. The sun's perimeter is about 2,713,406 miles (4,366,813 km).

14 Sun Facts

1. **The Sun Accounts For 99.86% Of The Mass In The Solar System.** It has a mass of around 330,000 times that of Earth. It is three quarters hydrogen and most of its remaining mass is helium.

2. **Over One Million Earth's Could Fit Inside The Sun.** If you were to fill a hollow Sun with spherical Earths, somewhere around 960,000 would fit inside. However, if you, squashed those Earths to ensure there was no wasted space then you could fit 1,300,000 Earths inside the Sun. The surface area of the Sun is 11,990 times that of Earth.

3. **One Day The Sun Will Consume The Earth.** The Sun will continue to burn for about 130 million years after it burns through all of its hydrogen, instead burning helium. During this time it will expand to such a size that it will engulf Mercury, Venus, and Earth. When it reaches this point, it will have become a red giant star.

4. **The Energy Created By The Sun's Core Is Nuclear Fusion.** This huge amount of energy is produced when four hydrogen nuclei are combined into one helium nucleus.

5. **The Sun Is Almost A Perfect Sphere.** Considering the sheer size of the Sun, there is only a 10 km difference in its polar and equatorial diameters – this makes it the closest thing to a perfect sphere observed in nature.

6. **The Sun Is Travelling At 220 Km Per Second.** It is around 24,000-26,000 light-years from the galactic center and it takes the Sun approximately 225-250 million years to complete one orbit of the center of the Milky Way.

7. **The Sun Will Eventually Be About The Size Of Earth.** Once the Sun has completed its red giant phase, it will collapse. It's huge mass will be retained, but it will have a volume similar to that of Earth. When that happens, it will be known as a white dwarf.

8. **It Takes Eight Minutes For Light Reach Earth From The Sun.** The average distance from the Sun to the Earth is about 150 million km. Light travels at 300,000

km per second so dividing one by the other gives you 500 seconds – eight minutes and twenty seconds.

9. **The Sun Is Halfway Through Its Life span. At 4.5 Billion Years Old.** The Sun has burned off around half of its hydrogen stores and has enough left to continue burning hydrogen for another 5 billion years. Currently the Sun is a yellow dwarf star.

10. **The Sun Has A Powerful Magnetic Field.** When magnetic energy is released by the Sun during magnetic storms, solar flares occur which we see on Earth as sunspots. Sunspots are dark areas on the Sun's surface caused by magnetic variations. The reason they appear dark is due to their temperature being much lower than surrounding areas.

11. **Temperatures Inside The Sun Can Reach 15 Million Degrees Celsius.** Energy is generated through nuclear fusion in the Sun's core – this is when hydrogen converts to helium – and because objects generally expand, the Sun would explode like an enormous bomb if it wasn't for it's tremendous gravitational pull.

12. **The Sun Generates Solar Winds.** These are ejections of plasma (extremely hot charged particles) that originate

in the layer of the Sun know as the corona and they can travel through the solar system at up to 450 km per second.

13. **The Sun Is Classified As A Yellow Dwarf Star.** It is a main sequence star with surface temperatures between 5,000 and 5,700 degrees celsius (9,000 and 10,300 degrees fahrenheit).

14. **The Aurora Borealis And Aurora Australis Are Caused By The Interaction Of Solar Winds With Earth's Atmosphere.**

While our Sun does not have a official scientific name, it does have another common name: Sol. This name originates from the ancient Roman's god of the Sun, Sol. This alternate name is where we get the term "solar system," which literally means system of the Sun.

Chapter 2

Sun Damages

Causes To Protect

It is very common to see people with sun damaged skin also known as photo damage, this is caused by the accumulation of sun exposure in your life. When the chronic photo damage changes the skin appearance it is called photo aging. The UVA rays of the sun are the major cause of skin aging.

The common signs of sun damage are fine lines, wrinkles, age spots, brown spots, increased pigmentation, etc. The areas more affected are the face, chest and the hands. Over exposure can even produce skin cancer and also can produce a yellowish chicken skin look.

Causes Of Sun Damage

As stated earlier, sun's ultraviolet radiation is responsible for a majority of skin conditions. These rays can be classified into three bands, UVA, UVB, and UVC. The ozone layer plays a crucial role in absorbing and reducing the intensity of incident

UV rays. The ozone-depleting chemicals are gradually stealing away the effectiveness of the screen. As the result, 95 percent of the incident UVA and 5 percent of UVB is able to reach the Earth's surface and cause extensive skin damage.

UVA (380-400nm) is less powerful, but it penetrates deeper into the skin and leads to premature aging of the skin. UVB (280-380nm) rays, on the other hand, chiefly results in sunburns and a variety of skin cancers. Research studies have revealed that UVA can augment the carcinogenic effects of UVB. UVC (100-280nm) rays are mostly absorbed by the ozone layer, ordinary air, and dead skin on the human body. Hence, they are not as damaging as the other two types of ultraviolet radiation.

Protecting from Young

**"If you teach kids early on to protect their skin,
they'll continue as they get older,"**

Protecting children is paramount – five severe sunburns before the age of 18 can double your risk of developing melanoma skin cancer in later life – but be careful with babies. "Babies under six months should not have sunscreen applied to them because of their skin is too thin and sensitive to the chemicals, Toy sunglasses wore in the sun may be worse for your baby's eyes than nothing at all. Toy sunglasses simply shade baby's eyes, making her pupils larger and actually allowing more damaging rays to reach the inside of the eye. Furthermore, it is believed that approximately 50 to 75 percent of a person's lifetime sun exposure occurs before the age of 20 years. If proper precautions aren't taken, the probability of developing sun-related diseases increases exponentially.

Types Of Sun Damage

Unprotected sun exposure can cause one or more of the following skin conditions.

1. **Irregular pigmentation-** In a bid to protect itself from the sun, the skin intensifies the production of melanin. This dark brown pigment gives the skin a peculiar tan. Uneven melanin production causes irregular pigmentation of the skin.

2. **Age spots-** Age spots, also called liver spots, appear when excessive pigmentation occurs due to overexposure to the sun.

3. **Solar elastosis-** Ultraviolet radiation can smash up the collagen and elastin fibers. In the absence of supporting connective tissue, the skin loses its elasticity and becomes wrinkled. This condition is called solar elastosis.

4. **Melasma-** Also known as pregnancy mask, melasma is prevalent in women who are either pregnant or take oral contraceptives. Excessive sun exposure aggravates the condition.

5. **Poikiloderma-** It is characterized by reddish-brown pigmentation, which appears in those areas of the body that are overexposed to the sun.

6. **Solar keratoses-** These are rough, scaly pink or brown patches commonly found on the face, ears and hands. If left untreated, they can progress to squamous cell carcinoma.

7. **Lentigo maligna-** It usually develops in those areas of the body that are exposed to the sun for a long period of time. In the initial stages, it appears as a small, dark spot. Gradually, it darkens and grows in size.

8. **Farmer's lips-** It is a precancerous condition in which the lips become dry and scaly.

9. **Squamous cell carcinoma-** It appears as a scaly red nodule on those areas of the body that are chronically exposed to the sun such as head, lips and hand.

10. **Bowen disease-** It is non-invasive cancer of the squamous cells.

11. **Basal cell carcinoma-** It is the most common type of skin cancer. It appears as a flat, scaly ulcerated area.

12. **Melanoma-** Most of the deaths related to skin cancer are caused by melanoma. It appears as asymmetrical freckles, lumps or moles.

Symptoms:

- Exceptionally dry skin that remains as such despite of using over-the-counter ointments and lotions

- Scaly nodules or patches that literally refuse to heal

- Painful sunburns with swelling and blisters

- Changes in shape and color of existing moles or appearance of lesions or lumps

Remember, Sun Damage Should Never Be Ignored, Lack Of immediate Care Can Cause Skin Cancer.

Cancer And Melanoma

Skin cancers are broadly divided into two types- Melanoma and non-melanoma. Melanoma is the most deadly of skin cancers. The three major skin cancers that are diagnosed in almost all the cases are- Basal Cell Carcinoma, Squamous Cell Carcinoma, and Melanoma. All these cancers are named after the type of cell in which they begin. Thus Basal Cell Carcinoma begins in the skin cells located in the lowest layer of epidermis, which is called the basal layer. Squamous Cell Carcinoma develops from the upper layer of the epidermis named squamous layer and Melanoma begins from the melanocytes. Melanocytes are the cells that give skin its color.

Basal Cell Cancer

It is one the most frequently diagnosed skin cancers. It affects the basal cells, which are located in the bottom layer of the epidermis. Malignant cells proliferate excessively from the epidermis resulting in a tumor. The incidence of basal cell cancer increases with age. Almost all people diagnosed with basal cell carcinoma can expect to live at least another 5 years.

Though it generally does, not spread to distant sites (metastasize), and is, therefore, less fatal. Basal cell carcinoma can invade normal tissue and damage deeper tissues of muscles and bones, and disfigure the skin. On its return, Basal cell carcinoma can be more aggressive. During recurrence it may grow faster and cause more tissue damage.

Squamous Cell Cancer

This type of cancer involves the malignancy and proliferation of squamous (flat, scaly) cells. The squamous cell or keratinocyte is the most abundant cell in the epidermis. Cutaneous squamous cell carcinoma is usually localized, but it can spread (metastasize). It is easily treated and cured when confined to the skin. Most cutaneous SCC develops in individuals with known factors, such as excessive exposure to the sun.

What is Melanoma?

Melanoma is a less common type of skin cancer. However, it is mostly associated with deaths due to skin cancer. This type of cancer is caused by melanocytes. These are normal cells present in the skin which give the dark pigmentation of the skin.

Causes of Melanoma

The exact cause of melanoma is still not determined. Genetic cause has been implicated. Several genes have been isolated being identified as the main cause as to why only certain people are affected by this cancer. A number of mutations in the genetic structure of individuals have been attributed as the primary causes for the predominance of melanoma in certain ethnic group of people. Ultra violet radiation from the sun or from tanning beds is the other factor which can trigger melanoma.

Diagnosis

Currently melanoma is diagnosed only after it becomes visible to the naked eyes. Five characteristics signs and symptom associated with melanoma include:

1. Irregular Or Asymmetrical Lesion On The Skin Surface or under the nails.

2. Skin Lesions Which Are Enlarging In Size. These lesions can also become hard and can cause severe itching. Some melanomas can also give rise to pain.

3. Color Of The Melanoma Is Usually Multicolored. Other innocent skin lesion will either be black or brown however melanoma can have a mixture of colors.

4. Melanomas Tend To Be Bigger Than Anyother Lesion. This is due to the fact that the lesion is usually discovered after the melanoma has enlarged.

5. The Border Of This Skin Lesion Is Uneven. Normal skin lesions usually have a smooth and even border however melanoma has a rough border due to continuous spread on the skin's surface.

Prevention Of Melanoma

Many dermatologists around the world agree that minimizing the exposure to ultraviolet rays reduce the chances of activation of melanocytes. The simple steps like wearing long sleeved shirts when one goes out in the sun, or wearing a broad straw hat to protect the face and neck from long exposures to sun light can minimize the chances of having melanoma. In 2009 it was classified that tanning beds are carcinogenic, meaning cancer inducing instrument. Everyone should avoid using these beds often.

Treating Melanoma

Although the survival rate of people surviving from melanoma is not so high, various treatment modalities are available. This includes a surgical approach where the lesion will be completely excised from the skin. Following this, patients might have to undergo chemotherapy and radiotherapy depending on the stage of the cancer.

Chapter 3

Sunscreens Differences

How Do Sunscreens Work ?

From a very young age, I recall my mother applaying my brother and I with sunscreen to guard us from getting excessive sun burns. We'd be at the seashore with our sandcastle crumbling down and my mom would be there, adding one more application of sunscreen.

We didnt know then of course, jut how very important it was to guard our skin. I have light skin. And I do recall without sunscreen, my young skin would burn in under five minutes in the summer months. So, it had become critical that preventative action was applied. I am thankful that my mom was indeed wise in this manner. And though it has become a part of my sun regimen, I did not think much about what sunscreen was in fact and in what way it functioned up until numerous years back. I considered you might be curious too.

Exactly What Is Sunscreen?

Sunscreens are filters of Ultra Violet rays. They are used to filter only a part of these UV rays. By classification, all forms of sunscreen include active ingredients that either absorb or scatter and reflect UV rays that would otherwise enter into the skin and cause a sunburn. UV Natural sunscreen uses Zinc Oxide that is a reflector of both UVA and UVB Rays. One common misconception is when you put on sunscreen you'll be completely protected from the sun's harmful UVA and UVB rays and can't get a sunburn. This is just not true! Sunscreens only decrease the burning affect of UV rays you'll experience when you don't use it at all.

How Does Sunscreen Work?

Sunscreens are filters, not "blocks." Every one of them allow some UV rays through at differing levels showed by the SPF number. An SPF 30 sunscreen will permit 1/30th of the UV rays to pass through it in the equivalent length of time as it would with no sunscreen whatsoever. It's important to totally understand this definition so you're able to understand how a sunscreen functions. If you use an SPF 30 sunscreen it will take

30 times as long for the sun burning dose of UV rays to accumulate.

Furthermore, be aware that sunburn might take hours to actually show-up on the skin. Therefore If you receive enough UV rays to produce a sunburn, no sunscreen or re-application is going to protect against this effect. This is the reason it is important to apply your sunscreen BEFORE sun exposure. Repeated applications of sunscreen are only maintenance of the original application. It does not restart your time in the sun; it just provides the original application an extra boost, improving its performance.

Tests completed by the testing facility at UV Natural sunscreen indicates that it will take from 6 to 10 minutes to begin to receive burning from the sun without protection. This is dependent upon different skin types and also changes for different regions and seasons.

Putting on an SPF 30 product for instance, in theory provides you with 30 times the protection before burning occurs. Re-application is needed and advised every 2 hours. Activities that cause sweating, towel drying, and lengthy amounts of time in the water are generally reasons to reapply sunscreen.

In the UK, it's illegal to label an SPF higher than 50 because, beyond SPF 30, there is a little jump in protection. "SPF 30 will protect against 98 percent of the sun's UVB wavelength rays and SPF 50 will protect against about 98.8 percent," says Dr. Lowe. That means if you apply enough SPF 30, you'll get the right amount.

For example a cream with SPF 60 will not provides double the protection of an SPF 30. This is exactly why the FDA is putting a cap on high SPF. SPF 30 provides skin with 98% protection, where as SPF 60 provides skin with 98-98.6% protection. There is less than 1.6% difference in protection factor. An SPF 60+ needs more chemicals to achieve a higher SPF, potentially putting more toxins in your body.

We know that sunlight damages the skin because of UVB, the rays that cause sunburn and can lead to skin cancer, and UVA rays, present even on cloudy days, which penetrate deep below the skin, causing premature aging and are also linked to melanoma. A Suncream's SPF rating relates to protection from UVB, while its star rating – five being the highest – relates to UVA protection. However, UV light makes up only about seven percent of the sun's rays. About 50 percent of it is made of infrared-A (IR-A) light. "IR-A appears to induce free radical formation and penetrate the skin, causing damage that can potentially lead to skin aging. Traditional sun creams do not generally have IR-A protection,"

Sunscreens come in different forms. You can choose from creams, lotions, moisturizers, sprays, sticks, and gel. Aside from their forms, they can also be categorized according to how they protect your skin from the sun and the ingredients they are made of.

You may not know this, but there are actually two different types of sunscreen: mineral and chemical. "Mineral sunscreens are 'physical' sunscreens and contain zinc or titanium,". They deflect the sun's rays, instead of absorbing them, like chemical sunscreens do. Both are FDA-approved, but many people may prefer mineral sunscreens because of they're made with more natural ingredients.

Mineral Vs Chemical Sunscreens ?

What Are Physical/Mineral Sunscreens ?

There are two types of physical sunscreens namely zinc oxide and titanium dioxide. Physical sunblocks protects the skin by reflecting or scattering the sun's UV rays before it even penetrates in the skin. They are not absorbed by the skin so they last longer and can work as soon as they are applied. Both zinc oxide and titanium dioxide are known to be gentle enough for everyday use, safe for babies as well. They only stay on top of the skin hence they rarely cause skin irritation or trigger allergies. It can be applied three times a day like in the morning, noon, and afternoon.

What Is Good About Mineral/Physical Sunscreens:

1. **Offers protection against both UVA and UVB rays** and is naturally broad spectrum.

2. **Better for those with heat-activated skin** (like those with rosacea and redness) since it deflects the heat and energy given off by the sun away from the skin.

3. **Protects from the sun as soon as it's applied,** no wait needed.

4. **Lasts longer when in direct UV light** (but NOT when doing physical activities that cause the skin to get wet or sweat).

5. **Less likely to cause a stinging irritation** on the skin, making it better for sensitive skin.

What Is Bad About Physical Sunscreens:

1. **Can rub off,** sweat off and rinse off easily, meaning more frequent reapplication when outdoors is needed.

2. **May leave a white-ish cast** on the skin, making some formulas incompatible for medium to dark skin tones.

3. **Can create an occlusive film,** which results in increased perspiration during physical activities and, therefore, causes it to wear off more quickly.

4. **Can be thicker,** which will require more effort to rub on the skin.

5. **Can be less protective if not applied generously** and accurately since UV light can get between the sunscreen molecules and get into the skin

Chemical Sunscreens

Unlike physical sunscreens, chemical sunscreens penetrate the skin and are made of several active ingredients. Several chemicals are combined and each one blocks a different region of UV ray. A sunscreen is labeled as "broad spectrum" when it has all the chemicals needed to protect the skin from the harmful rays of the sun. Most chemical sunscreens work against UVB and UVA rays and may also contain a physical blocking agent like zinc oxide, titanium dioxide, or Avobenzone.

What Is Good About Chemical Sunscreens:

1. **Tends to be thinner** and, therefore, spreads more easily on the skin, making it more wearable for daily use.

2. **Less is needed to protect the skin** because there is no risk of no spaces between the sunscreen molecules after application.

3. **The Formula is easier to add additional treatment ingredients,** such as peptides and enzymes, which offer other skin benefits.

What Is Bad About Chemical Sunscreens:

1. **Can possibly cause an increase in existing brown spots and discoloration** due to a higher internal skin temperature (Yes, over-heated skin can make brown spots worse.

2. **Requires about 20 minutes after application before it begins to work.**

3. **Increased chance of irritation and stinging** (especially for those who have dry skin with a damaged moisture barrier) due to the multiple ingredients combined in order to achieve broad spectrum UVA and UVB protection.

4. **The higher the SPF** (such as formulas of SPF 50 or greater), **the higher the risk of irritation for sensitive skin types.**

5. **The protection it offers gets used up more quickly when in direct UV light,** so reapplication must be more frequent.

6. **Increased chance of redness for rosacea-prone skin types** because it changes UV rays into heat which can couse red flushing on the face.

7. **May clog the pores for oily skin types.**

8. **Can cause stinging if it drips into the eyes from sweat.**

Do BB And CC Creams really works ?

BB and CC creams are not adequate for use in intense sunlight for long periods. Some of them may help protect skin from the sun's damaging ultraviolet radiation during low-exposure activities such as driving, walking between shaded areas or indoors, but they will not shield your skin from harmful rays if you are outside for a longer time span or if you will be in intense sunlight.

BB mean 'beauty balm' at the same time as CC way 'complexion corrector' or 'colour and accurate.' A beauty balm gives the user with instantaneous sheer coverage in addition to SPF. The complexion corrector offers the user with help to cope with any problems of redness or pale complexion in addition to benefits of anti-Aging.

The Difference Between BB And CC

BB creams are more moisturizing and creamy than CC Creams. The word BB stands for beauty balm or blemish balm and does what its name suggests. It imparts a full insurance to the face with SPF and antioxidant properties. It offers a smooth and wonderful finish, without the cakey finish of foundations. It has a mild cover than regular foundations however it is a bit heavy than regular moisturizers. It imparts a dewy finish and is an awesome product for normal to dry skin.

CC lotions are light-weight in texture and have a fast absorbing assets. not like BB creams, CC lotions are oil free and consequently, best for shiny and acne susceptible pores and skin. CC lotions have a lighter insurance and recognition on skin correction inclusive of any redness or sallowness. It evens out the pores and skin and offers it a corrected perfect finish. They normally have a sophisticated formula that makes them speedy absorbing with mild diffusing debris and antioxidants that immediately corrects the pores and skin.

Is My Make Up Enough As Sun Protection ?

Make up of all kinds and forms gives very good protection against the sun when using them on top of a sun screen or sun block. They usually contain maximum SPF 15 that is not considered as a satisfactory sun protection by itself.

Above All, Don't Fall Into The Trap Of Letting Your Make Up, BB And CC Cream Give You A False Sense

Of Security. You Need To Take Other Sun Protection Measures Like A Regular Sun Screen Seek The Shade.

Sport And Water Resistant Or Waterproof Sunblocks

Since the sun's UV rays can still pass through water, you still need sunscreen when you go swimming. Water resistant sunblocks are especially designed for those who are involved in water sports. There is, however, a difference between a water resistant sunblock and a waterproof sunblock. The first can maintain its SPF level after 40 minutes under the water while the latter maintains the SPF level after 80 minutes of being immersed in water. A waterproof sunscreen stays and protects longer than a water resistant sunscreen. Check the labels to ensure that you got what you want.

sports sunscreens are usually tested to measure how water resistant a formula is before its Sun Protection Factor (SPF) starts to wear off. While such testing is tailored for prolonged water immersion, such as sunscreen for swimmers, it can also reflect sweat resistance.sport sunscreen for swimmers. As defined by Mayo Clinic, "the term water resistant means that the SPF is maintained for up to 40 minutes while swimming or sweating. Very water resistant means the SPF is maintained for 80 minutes."

In addition to athletes, sport sunscreen is often an appropriate option for anyone looking to get wet, work-up a sweat, or enjoy several hours of sun exposure. Offering more advanced, broad-spectrum protection capabilities, a good sport sunscreen is often the better choice versus regular sports sunscreen.

What Kind Of Sun Protection To Choose?

Depending on the country you live in and how much sun exposure you get, it is always recommended to use a few kinds of protection mixed together. For the summer it is good to use a broad spectrum sun screen with SPF 30 that contains the mineral ingredients and the chemical ones.

Good companies make excellent formulas that are very protective but not harsh on the skin and are suitable also for babies. One layer is never enough and for good lasting protection it is recommended to add after the layer of protection a layer of BB or CC cream and then even make up and powder that gives extra protection and bind all the protective layers together, mixing a few products for protection gives the best tight protection to the skin of the face.

If you work outside you can incorporate a sports sun block and add a thin or thick layer after your regular sun screen and then add some color with BB or make up so it want look so white. The combinations are endless but the important thing is to use not just one layer of protection but numerous layers as needed and repeating putting them several times a day especially when outside.

Chapter 4

Protect From The Sun

Be Responsible About Your Skin

Only about 14 percent of men and 30 percent of women report wearing sunscreen. Even when they do, they use around half what they need. You needs two milligrams of sun cream per centimeter squared of skin. you don't have to be out sunbathing from sun-up to sun-down to increase your chances of damaging your skin. Even overcast days can contribute to the tanning and eventual premature aging process of your skin - no matter whether you've got dark or extremely fair skin.

Whilst nobody would recommend you cover yourself up completely and lock yourself indoors there are many, very simple precautions you can take to help protect your skin from the affects of the sun.

If you plan on being outside for a extended amount of time, here are tips to learn before you burn:

10 Tips To Protect Yourself From The Sun

1. **Use sunscreen with a Sun Protection Factor (SPF) of at least 30.** Make sure it is water-resistant and reapply every two hours, especially after swimming or sweating.

2. **Apply sunscreen 30 minutes before going outside** so your skin has time to absorb it.

3. **Be generous in application of sunscreen.** An ounce of sunscreen should cover the face, neck, arms and legs of the average adult.

4. **Wear protective clothing,** like hats, sunglasses, long-sleeved shirts, and pants.

5. **Seek shade when possible,** especially during the hours of 10:00 am to 4:00 pm when the sun's rays are strongest.

6. **Avoid tanning beds** as ultraviolet light can cause skin cancer and wrinkling. Use a self-tanning product but use sunscreen with it.

7. **Protect children by reapplying sunscreen often** with an SPF of at least 30, having them play in the shade and wear protective clothing.

8. **Babies under the age of 6 months should never be in direct sunlight** and should always wear an hat and clothing that protects them from UV rays.

9. **Adults should perform regular self-exams.** It is an easy way to detect abnormalities and skin moles.

10. **Talk to your dermatologist and have a complete body scan once a year.**

More About Staying In The Shade

Seeking shade whenever possible is the best sun protection and sometimes it is the smartest option when UV levels are extreme. Shade, though, will not give total protection. It is still possible to be exposed to UV rays that bounce off of reflective surfaces such as water, ice, show and sand. Be mindful of this if you are sitting under an umbrella but are near one of these reflective surfaces like a swimming pool.

It is important to remember that there is no single product that will protect 100 percent against damaging UV rays. Combine sun protective products with broad-spectrum sunscreen and seek shade when possible to achieve maximum protection. Sun safety should be a regimen that is practiced daily.

Chapter 5

Vitamin D Myth And Truth

What Is Vitamin D?

Vitamin D is fat-soluble (it is stored in fatty tissues and stays in your body longer), we need vitamin D to keep normal levels of calcium and phosphorus in our blood. The main thing we know about vitamin D is that it helps to keep our bones strong.

A recent study showed that getting enough vitamin D may prevent diabetes. Further studies have shown that most Americans don't get enough vitamin D which promotes calcium absorption in the gut and maintains adequate serum calcium and phosphate concentrations to enable normal mineralization of bone and to prevent hypocalcemic tetany.

Vitamin D is also needed for bone growth and bone remodeling by osteoblasts and osteoclasts. Without sufficient vitamin D, bones can become thin and brittle. Vitamin D sufficiency prevents rickets in children and osteomalacia in adults. Together with calcium, vitamin D also helps protect older adults from osteoporosis.

There Are Two Forms Of Vitamin D In Nature:

- ✓ **Vitamin D2 (ergocalciferol):** found in some mushrooms.

- ✓ **Vitamin D3 (cholecalciferol):** found in oily fish, fish liver oil and egg yolks.

D3 is the more powerful of the two types, and raises blood levels of vitamin D almost twice as much as D2.

Large amounts of vitamin D can also be made in your skin when it is exposed to UV-rays from sunlight. Any excess vitamin D is stored in your body fat for later use.

Every cell in your body has a receptor for vitamin D. This vitamin is involved in many processes, including bone health, immune system function and protection against cancer

The Main Sources Of Vitamin D

Our body creates vitamin D from direct sunlight on our skin when we are outdoors. From about late March/early April to the end of September, most people should be able to get all the vitamin D we need from sunlight. We also get some vitamin D from a small number of foods, including oily fish such as salmon, mackerel, herring and sardines, as well as red meat and eggs. Vitamin D is also added to all infant formula milk, as well as some breakfast cereals, fat spreads and non-dairy milk alternatives. The amounts added to these products can vary and may only be added in small amounts. Manufacturers must by law add vitamin D to infant formula milk and Another source of vitamin D is dietary supplements.

We Can Get Vitamin D From:

✓ **Sun exposure.**

✓ **Foods that contain vitamin D.**

✓ **Supplements.**

Vitamin D intake is generally quite low, since very few foods contain significant amounts. Foods that do contain vitamin D includes fatty fish like salmon, as well as fish liver oils. Egg yolks also contain small amounts, and in some countries milk and cereals are enriched with vitamin D. However, supplements are also widely available, and are both safe and effective.

Symptoms And Health Risks
Of Vitamin D Deficiency

Symptoms of bone pain and muscle weakness can mean you have a vitamin D deficiency. However, for many people, the symptoms are subtle. Yet, even without symptoms, too little vitamin D can pose health risks. Low blood levels of the vitamin have been associated with the following:

- ✓ **Increased risk of death from cardiovascular disease**

- ✓ **Cognitive impairment in older adults**

- ✓ **Severe asthma in children**

- ✓ **Cancer**

Research suggests that vitamin D could play a role in the prevention and treatment of a number of different conditions, including type1 and type 2 diabetes, hypertension, glucose intolerance, and multiple sclerosis.

The Purpose Of Vitamin D In The Body

Vitamin D serves several important functions in the body. These includes:

- ✓ **promoting calcium absorption**
- ✓ **maintaining normal calcium and phosphate levels**
- ✓ **promoting bone and cell growth**
- ✓ **reducing inflammation**

Causes Of Vitamin D Deficiency

Vitamin D deficiency can occur for a number of reasons:

You Don't Consume The Recommended Levels Of The Vitamin Over Time- This is likely if you follow a strict vegan diet, because most of the natural sources are animal-based, including fish and fish oils, egg yolks, fortified milk, and beef liver.

Your Exposure To Sunlight Is Limited- Because the body makes vitamin D when your skin is exposed to sunlight, you may be at risk of deficiency if you are homebound, live in northern latitudes, wear long robes or head coverings for religious reasons, or have an occupation that prevents sun exposure.

You Have Dark Skin- The pigment melanin reduces the skin's ability to make vitamin D in response to sunlight exposure. Some studies show that older adults with darker skin are at high risk of vitamin D deficiency.

Your Kidneys Cannot Convert Vitamin D To Its Active Form- As people age, their kidneys are less able to convert vitamin D to its active form, thus increasing their risk of vitamin D deficiency.

Your Digestive Tract Cannot Adequately Absorb Vitamin D- Certain medical problems, including Crohn's disease, cystic fibrosis, and celiac disease, can affect your intestine's ability to absorb vitamin D from the food you eat.

You Are Obese. Vitamin D Is Extracted From The Blood By Fat Cells- altering its release into the circulation. People with a body mass index of 30 or greater often has low blood levels of vitamin D.

Tests For Vitamin D Deficiency

The most accurate way to measure how much vitamin D is in your body is the 25-hydroxy vitamin D blood test. A-level of 20 nanograms/milliliter to 50 ng/mL is considered adequate for healthy people. A-level less than 12 ng/mL indicates vitamin D deficiency.

Treatment For Vitamin D Deficiency

Treatment for vitamin D deficiency involves getting more vitamin D through diet and supplements. Although there is no consensus on vitamin D levels required for optimal health and it likely differs depending on age and health conditions a concentration of less than 20 nanograms per milliliter is generally considered inadequate, requiring treatment.

Guidelines from the Institute of Medicine increased the recommended dietary allowance (RDA) of vitamin D to 600 international units (IU) for everyone ages 1-70, and raised it to 800 IU for adults older than age 70 to optimize bone health.

The safe upper limit was also raised to 4,000 IU. Doctors may prescribe more than 4,000 IU to correct a vitamin D deficiency.

If you don't spend much time in the sun or always are careful to cover your skin (sunscreen inhibits vitamin D production), you should speak to your doctor about taking a vitamin D supplement, particularly if you have risk factors for vitamin D deficiency.

How Much Vitamin D Should Children Take?

According to to the NIH, AI for children from birth until 5 years of age should take 5 mcg per day (200 IU).

How Much Vitamin D Should Adults Take?

According to the National Institutes of Health (NIH), the daily Adequate Intake (AI) for adults is 5 mcg (200 IU) daily for males, female, and pregnant/lactating women under the age of 50. People 50 to 70 years old should get 10 mcg daily (400 IU) daily, and those over 70 should get 15 mcg daily (600 IU). Based on recent research, Dr. Weil recommends 2,000 IU of vitamin D per day. Look for supplements that provide D3 (cholecalciferol) rather than D2 (ergocalciferol). Anyone with vitamin D deficiencies should discuss intake levels with his or her physician.

What Are Some Vitamin D Foods?

It isn't easy to get enough vitamin D from your diet. While fortified vitamin D foods such as milk and cereals are available, most provide vitamin D2, a form which is much less well-utilized by the body than D3. Good dietary sources include fortified foods, eggs, salmon, tuna, mackerel and sardines. Since sunlight causes our bodies to make vitamin D, daily exposure is helpful. A helpful rule: estimate the amount of time it would take for your skin to turn pink – or slightly, but noticeably darker in the sun. Then reduce that time by 50 percent if you have fair skin, 25 percent for darker skin, and get that amount of exposure between 11 a.m. and 3 p.m. two to three times per week.

How Much Is Too Much?

Information about vitamin D overdose is outdated, and toxicity is extremely rare.

It is associated with dangerously high amounts of calcium and phosphates in the blood, along with low levels of parathyroid hormone. This is typically only seen in individuals who have accidentally or intentionally taken extremely high doses of vitamin D for long periods of time, such as 50,000–1 million IU/day for months.

The upper level of harmless intake is set at 4000 IU, or 100 micrograms, per day. However, up to 10,000 IU per day has not been shown to cause harm to healthy individuals.

That being said, very few people actually need more than 4000 IU a day. A study of 17 thousand people taking varying doses of vitamin D, up to 20,000 IU/day, did not demonstrate any signs of toxicity. Their blood levels were still lower than the upper range of normal, which is 100 ng/ml, or 250 nmol/l.

Also, **it is not possible to overdose on vitamin D from sunlight.** Keep in mind that although large doses are unlikely to cause harm or toxicity, they may be completely unnecessary.

Chapter 6

Correct Sun Damage

Start Treating Your Skin Nice

Are you worried about the permanent effects of sun damage? You should be. The ultraviolet rays of the sun can easily weaken skin cells and tissues. Chronic exposure to UV rays can accelerate the aging process of the integumentary system. In worse cases, this might even trigger skin cancer, Unfortunately, sun damage isn't something that just happens to sun worshipers, even a few minutes of exposed unprotected skin can cause problems. Another big culprit is childhood burns which can wreak havoc years after the initial burn. Skin issues from sun exposure can start earlier than you think.

How to know If Your Skin Is Damaged Because Of The Sun?

1. **Darkening Of Skin Tone -** According to experts, our integumentary system tends to produce more melanin

as a way of reversing the negative effects of ultraviolet rays. Melanin is the pigment that gives our skin a darker color.

2. **Peeling -** Skin peeling usually happens if your skin has been damaged severely. The topmost layers of the skin are damaged beyond repair. They are peeled off to reveal younger skin underneath.

3. **Dryness Of The Dermis-** If your dermis feels rough, dry and tight, it is an indication of sun damage. Your skin no longer has the essential moisture and lipids that sustain it and keep it moist.

Stop And Reverse Sun Damage

1. **Exfoliate and Peel-** The buildup of stratum corneum (the dead, outermost skin cell layer) can make skin appear blotchy and uneven. Also, remnants of self-tanning products can collect in typically dry areas (such as the elbows), causing the skin to lose its luster and appear "dirty." Loofahs, scrubs, alpha hydroxy acid (AHA) cleansers, and home microdermabrasion kits (in which tiny crystals are sprayed on the skin) can remove dead skin cells, leaving skin looking smoother.

2. **Use Sunscreen With An SPF Of 30 Or Higher-** Sunscreen is one of the keys to radiant, youthful-looking skin. Daily use may even lower your long-term risk of skin cancer. By reducing your daily sun exposure, sunscreen allows your skin time to heal and your immune system the chance to repair some existing damage.

3. **Hydrate-** Summer exposure to sun, chlorine, and salt water can dry out your skin - even the heels of your feet can be affected. Try a hand and body cream, and, for the heels, a moisturizing foot cream. A moisturizer with AHA or facial serum with hyaluronic acid can plump up dry skin around the eyes, making skin instantly appear less wrinkled. Continued uses may help stimulate the production of new collagen, a protein that helps give skin its texture and appearance.

4. **Visit A Dermatologist -** Professional laser treatments can improve everything from blotchiness and discoloration to wrinkles. Peelings are one of the best solutions to sun damages, Medium to deep peelings can remove scaly patches of actinic keratoses from your skin.

5. **Try Intensed PulseD Light (IPL)-** Light treatments are special light bulbs that help to light pigmentation, you can find some home units in the market. IPL can help promote collagen production, reduce fine lines and wrinkles, and improve acne.

6. **Lightening Creams And Retinol –** Light the brown spots with Skin lightener does not actually make the skin white; it simply helps to lighten accumulations of unwanted color. It is recommended to us Professional cosmetic products that contains kojic acid in combination with hydroquinone, Retinol and AHA and BHA Creams, which is useful for stubborn brown spots and blotchy brown discoloration.

7. **Use The Layer Syatem -** The layer system is the most comprehensive cosmetic system to treat the skin from sun damage, pigmentation, skin spots, wrinkels and Anti-Aging all integrated to one working system.

Chapter 7

Build A Relationship With The Sun

Enjoy The Sun

Humans have had a natural relationship with the sun since far before sunscreen came along a relationship based on common sense, intuition, and being present by listening to one's own body.

If it's not a plant, I'm just not going to want to put it on my skin every day. However, summer has been part of a bigger journey for me in strengthening my own relationship with the sun. It's starting to sink in that what we get from the sun is far more beneficial than the fear the billion dollar sunscreen industry has installed in us. It's easy for me to experiment with my own relationship with the sun, mostly because of the knowledge I have about ingredients and chemical reactions within our skin. I typically work indoors, and very rarely get my recommended outdoor vitamin D time. Then a recent trip to India truly tested the health of my skin and body it also really tested our Sun Facial Serum, as well as my trusty Badger SPF 30. I would love to share a bit of my knowledge with you so that you can begin to conquer your fear of the sun as well.

Strategies For Safe And Healthy Sun Exposure

1. **Nutritional Sunscreen-** What we ingest determines how our skin responds to sunlight. Skin cells must be strengthened and nourished internally with real food and water to receive the full benefit of interacting with the sun. We can create an internal SPF with an antioxidant-rich diet of sun-grown foods, herbs, and fats loaded with nutrients. The powerhouse antioxidants in foods include: Lycopene in fresh tomatoes, Glutathione in grass fed meat, Alpha-Lipoic Acid found in broccoli, CoQ10 in nuts, Resveratrol in grapes and cacao, Carotenoids in carrots and squash, Astaxanthin in wild salmon and of course Vitamin C in berries, citrus and certain herbs such as strawberry leaf. Our nutritional sunscreen must be 'applied' at every meal, all year long, to provide maximum benefits.

2. **Make Time For Your Sun Bath-** Start slowly but surely to exposure your skin to the sun. Melanin, the tanned-skin pigment, produced in the spring, prevents

sunburn in the summer. Melanin is our ancient biological mechanism of photo-protection designed exclusively to support our relationship with the sun. Melanin transforms 99.9% of absorbed UV radiation into heat that is easily dissipated, allowing us to avoid radiation damage that contributes to cell damage. The best time of day for sunning is morning to solar-noon. The amount of time you bathe in the sun depends on the condition of your skin and your natural skin pigmentation. If your skin starts to feel warm, seek shade. Start with a few minutes a day and build-up.

3. **Think Sunblock Or Barrier Instead Of Sunscreen-** Using a sunscreen stops the much-needed UVB rays from their important Vitamin D work. Most of the sunscreens on the market contain various suspicious chemicals with names beginning or ending with Methyl, Propyl, Butyl, Ethyl, Trieth, and/or Dieth. Why would you want to filter the glorious sunshine through a array of chemicals? Sunscreens create a false sense of security by disabling our skin's early warning system, the sunburn. By disabling this system we tend to stay too long in the sun, not only burning but struggling with heat exposure as well. Uncoated zinc

oxide effectively blocks and reflects, rather than absorbs, the sun's rays and it won't paint the skin white. Consider barrier clothing as a option for sun protection. Don't forget your hat!

4. **Sun Exposure And Eye Health-** Our eyes need the sunlight, too. When the full spectrum of light rays is absorbed in the retina, it sets in motion the hormones and neurochemicals that help us stay happy and healthy. This process works even if we are in the shade, but not if we are wearing sunglasses. Children also need to be outside in the sun for healthy eye development. Sunlight triggers dopamine production in the eye, which stimulates normal growth.

5. **Recover Your Skin-** The skin's outer layer is a thin coating of oils that provides natural anti-bacterial, anti-wrinkle, and sunscreen protection. Using synthetic lotions and creams, exfoliants and harsh soaps interfere with this sensitive layer. Using natural oils, plant-based extracts plus following a dry skin brush regiment will help nourish this layer and build its resiliency. Remember not to shower off after being in the sun, allow those great UVB rays to continue their vitamin D work as along as possible.

Experience The Sun

The sun's rays are not free radicals, but rather our body's inflammatory response to them that creates free radical stress. Your own body actually chooses how to chemically respond to the sun. Our body can respond to the sun as something damaging, and then our skin will inflame (sun burn & sun damage), or our healthy bodies can process the sun's rays with ease, and can even utilize them in a healthy way to make vitamin D.

The only sufficient source of vitamin D for us is the sun. Vitamin D deficiency has been linked to multiple cancers, depression, weight gain, heart disease, high blood pressure, osteoporosis, and the list goes on. Studies have shown that in general those who spend more time in the sun actually show less of an inflammatory response, and by far have less documented cases of skin cancer than those who spend little to no time in the sun. 20 – 40 minutes a day is what is healthy for our bodies, and that is 20 – 40 minutes without sunscreen. Sunscreen that blocks UVB rays actually blocks vitamin D production. UVB rays are the rays that are responsible for D production, as well as the rays that are responsible for the sun burn. UVA rays are the rays connected to melanoma –

however, it's when UVAs are isolated that they are the most harmful. Keep in mind the sun's strongest hours are between 10am – 4pm, so if you want to absorb some sun light with no sun screen do it before or after this hours. Also, start with 20 minutes, and work your way up to 40. Sea Weed is good for you, but you would not eat 3 pounds of it! Everything in moderation, and do your best to listen to your own body and intuition. Wear hats and seek shade whenever necessary.

A Johns Hopkins study showcased that only those who were vitamin B and/or vitamin D deficient responded negatively to the sun's rays. And again, we are getting our vitamin D from the sun. It only makes sense that if we are in a board room 7 days a week, then head out on a boating adventure for the first time, our skin won't know what hit it!

Most of us are vitamin D deficient, from our lack of sun exposure. Other antioxidants, like vitamin B, we can get from our diet. Load up on those fruits and veggies and your body will be more prepared to handle those rays, without the help of sunscreen. Berries, kale, broccoli, cabbage, and turmeric are just a few specific foods to include in your summer diet. Our body even has a super antioxidant that will kick into high gear if we do start to inflame from the sun's rays. And those fruits and vegetables are a few ingredients that promote our body's own antioxidant response to kick on. On the flip side, if you're feeling under the weather or your immune system is lacking, that's the time to take the Mineral sunblock with you. Your body is less likely to handle inflammation and free radicals with ease if your immune system isn't at its best.

Most Sunscreen chemicals are truly the worst, and most of them are linked to cancer themselves so please don't swap one cancer for another. Non-nano zinc is the only FDA approved sunscreen drug that has not yet been linked to cancer, endocrine disruption, or serious health concerns, and is, therefore, the best option for those who need an additional sun block. I would recommend a good quolity sunblock SPF 30, for every day use and repeat applaying several time a day.

Natural Sun Screens

All high-quality unrefined oils like shea butter and coconut oil have varying levels of SPF and sun reflecting properties. In addition to those reflecting properties, some of these plants prevent sun damage in other ways like with antioxidants! Vitamin E and vitamin C actually neutralize the free-radical/inflammatory response our body can have from the sun. I would not count on this oils to fully protect from the sun but is good to use them regularly for skin health.

Your skin even strengthens with use of these antioxidants over time, to build up its own natural defense. In addition to that, healthy skin can even create its own antioxidants to help balance any free radical activity, as we mentioned above. However, skin that does this is seriously healthy skin! You have to feed your skin the same way you feed your body: with whole foods, super foods, and nutrient/antioxidant dense foods.

Sunscreen is needed in the world, especially because not all of us are fortunate enough to have an antioxidant-rich diet or an antioxidant-rich skin care routine. Most of us want to eat whatever we want, treat our bodies however we want, throw on some sunscreen and enjoy our vacation. Each person is different and has their own recipe for healthy summer skin. I hope some of this knowledge makes you feel more comfortable, and not too fearful to experiment with your own relationship with the sun.

CONCLUSION

The Sun is Fun and important for our health but we need to take the safe path and always cover our skin especially our face from the sun to avoid the signs of aging and skin damage. Don't be afraid of the sun but know the suns power and take measures to protect yourself by using different kinds of protection products.

The Sun provides us with vitamin D, the very necessary nutrient that has been linked to everything from keeping the immune system strong to cancer prevention. Getting a sufficient amount of the vitamin is important for normal growth and development of bones and teeth, as well as improved resistance against certain diseases. Remember that we cannot obtain vitamin D from the sun in winter dew to the angle of the sun's rays.

Absorbing the sun's rays in a healthful and safe way is crucial. There are definite risks in over exposure to the sun and heat of the sun. Knowing how to sun bathe in a way that builds wellness is the key.

Don't forget that more damage to all colors of skin and ages, we get from screens of the computers and all radiation around us so putting sunscreen every day is a must even to people who are working indoors like hospital staff and even teachers.

Thank you very much for reading the book. If you loved the book, I would appreciate it if you can write a review of the book for me. If you have any question about the book feel free to contact me at orilaor@outlook.com.

For 20$ Coupon for www.laorcare.com were you can find all the professional products to clear your Pigmentation, send the word: SUNISFUN to my mail.

With sincere love Ori Laor

www.ingramcontent.com/pod-product-compliance
Lightning Source LLC
Chambersburg PA
CBHW060804260726
48660CB00002B/762

Technology for Social Reform

Technology for Social Reform

Technology for Social Reform

Michael Holloway King, M.D.

Author of:
Overcoming Oppression: Your Guide to a New Life
Hide and Play Dead: From Memoir to Real-Time Healing

And the anthology series:
I Am Also a Voice: Creation of a Unique Racial Identity
Double Trouble: Creation of a Unique Sexual Identity
Individuation: Creation of a Unique Adult Identity
Contentment: Creation of a Unique Spiritual Identity

Technology for Social Reform

TABLE OF CONTENTS

Technology for Social Reform

Part One: Introduction and Overview

Social change is slow and seems to proceed by erratic quantum leaps, which may simulate the nature of human evolution itself.

Conversely, social structure has mutated in the relatively short span of two thousand years. And in the past one hundred years, the convergent forces of technology and population growth have propelled cultural shifts along an exponential curve of unbelievable speed.

When the issue of making a corresponding adjustment in our awareness of our *psychoemotional* nature is broached, it seems that we

1

are simultaneously rapacious for knowledge that will alter our behaviors *and* resistant to it. "Knowledge is power, but ignorance is bliss."

Something "new" is discovered about our age-old nature about every ten years, followed by a subjectively long lag before these revelations about our psychoemotional constitution reach the public. Yet, in a single human lifetime, change in beliefs about our genetic nature does happen.

Like a wave drifting to the shore of consensus, knowledge about our consciousness is like the hesitant path of social change in general, and follows a typical sequence from *visionary geniuses...* to *academic researchers...*to *mental health professionals...*to *physical medicine practitioners...*to *social engineers...*to *educators...*to *educated children*— Who must grow up, gain the right to vote, and finally legalize the knowledge so that it can be disseminated to the public at large.

My life's goal is to accelerate positive social change by providing precise psychoemotional tools that the reformist movement desperately needs to succeed.

True and transparent democracy, social justice and economic fairness are ready to return to America. The strategies and techniques that I provide are timely and appropriate for a majority-minority nation in a rapid change process.

I have developed several therapeutic processes designed to dismantle the subtle and usually subconscious yoke of social oppression in most people. The same approach can also produce leaders with powerful bio-physiological methods to catapult the resist movement *forwards* and *towards* true social equity.

The over-riding goal is to confer upon an expanding cell of people a sort of psychic immunity to the nefarious pressures of oppression. It is imperative to block the imposition of socioeconomic neoslavery upon docile masses.

This can only happen *peacefully* when lead by individuals who exemplify loving social engagement and cooperative action.

*

Technology for Social Reform

A full explanation of my *psychotherapeutic techniques* is covered in depth in my recently published book: "Overcoming Oppression: Your Guide to a New Life," and it is briefly reviewed in this paper. The associated *literary technology* and *biotechnologies* that I am using with success are also summarized here.

The outcomes of my work are to effectively treat persons who are sensitive to *shame induction*— or who are easily victimized by any form of *interpersonal abuse*, or have experienced psychological *trauma or PTSD*, or, by dint of these, are *easily oppressed*. The fact is that shame is ubiquitous, and most persons manifest the full psychobiology of oppression that blocks any individual effort to seek positive change in oneself, as well as in their social milieu.

This paper is uniquely designed to inform activists and social scientists about technology that can produce:

- An ability to spread the word about *neoslavery*, which is the most unifying concept for resistance, and which I fear may be our greatest social menace…

- A way to be tirelessly effective as social activists— armed only with new, peaceful weapons of the psyche…

- A hint of various strategies to quickly transmit liberating techniques to the still largely ignorant and oppressed masses— especially the invisible social underclass of our nation...

- Skills needed to more readily attract the support of socially conscious persons…

- A legacy and precedent of how to foment a non-violent revolution against the restrictive status quo of the corporate and social elite.

*

Preface from my book: "Overcoming Oppression"
The following narrative will give you a vivid overview of my entire treatise

We are at a crossroads of destiny on the little Planet Earth. Much of the world's population has become imprinted with toxic mind-sets,

3

and is vulnerable to the full range of shame—including abuse, trauma and social oppression. I only wish that all people, within the context of my narrative and the readers outside, will see the miasma of shame that we inhabit, and begin to dismantle the shackles that preclude our capacity for human love.

We swim in a polluted sea of shame, but most people are ignorant of its pervasive existence. We do not *see* shame—like fish that do not see water because it's everywhere, like air that is omnipresent but invisible, like dark matter which fills two-thirds of the universe but which cannot be found, like the strings of consciousness which connect all sapient beings but cannot be proved outside of mathematics, or like the concept of *infinity* that is real but can never be fully grasped by mortal beings. If we do not open our eyes and hearts to shame and become cognizant of its intrapsychic, biological and cultural effects, my inner voice shouts, "We will *all* perish. The time has come."

Yet there is still plenty of fresh water: One-by-one, every individual can escape the confines of self-oppression and literally evolve past the neurobiological constriction of toxic shame. In this book, I will demonstrate the full, blunt and brutal physical and psychological effects of the "dark side of the force" of shame—and then, I will present to you an exit from the cage.

One cannot understand social oppression without fully knowing the emotion of shame.

As you will see, shame is genetically wired into the human emotional brain for our survival. But if culturally perpetuated, *shame becomes toxic,* and alters the natural function and balance of the human brain. *Systematic abuse* maintains toxic shame in socialized, adult humans. When abuse occurs at a sufficient frequency or intensity, *trauma manifests* as fixed neurological malfunctions. And a population that is traumatized is *easily oppressed…*

We labor under the yolk of social oppression on a global scale, and social change is required. This happens naturally when enough people understand the urgent need for reform, and "Overcoming Oppression" is a grand leap towards educated action. Otherwise, the risk of violent resistance or revolution looms high, and the result is

4

often only a fleeting freedom that quickly reverts to *new* forms of oppression, perhaps *worse* than before.

This book is about how to heal and deliver you from shame and social oppression.

The structure of the book is designed to initiate the process of liberation from toxic shame, trauma and oppressive patterns from *many* different angles. Once the healing process presented in this book is learned, assimilated, and accommodated to your personal modifications, you will be desensitized to toxic shame—Or at least you will know what to do when toxic shame, abuse, trauma or re-traumatization occur. Ultimately, you will no longer be easily targeted for social oppression, whether from isolated human predators or from social institutions.

My goal in this book is to reveal shame and social oppression with graphic and naked exposure.

Others have already accomplished a concise and succinct depiction of psychological shame, and although they have made impressive strides, the "war on shame" is failing, as the few early theorists recede in defeat from a largely unaware public. Words, studies, references and brief coverage in the media do not apparently suffice. *Shock is needed!* I ardently aspire that the reader will feel the essence of shame, will feel uncomfortable and mildly stressed— and then be quickly nudged towards resolution of both shame and stress during the process of reading this text.

My method in this book is by metaphor, case histories, analogies from my biographical history and daily life, and copious exercises to raise the tide of awareness about shame by iconic, sensory-motor and subconscious learning methodologies. This book also offers a new and unprecedented literary path of personal engagement—a step-wise system by which the process of reading may alter the reader's neurobiology.

There is a pandemic prevalence of trauma in America, and globally.

We exist in a culture where stress, victimization and dysfunctional relationships have become common concepts that overflow in most persons' intimate discussions. The frequently touted percentage of Americans who feel abused is sky-high, with the widely accepted belief that eighty percent of the population is codependent or suffers from traumatic childrearing experiences.

Shame is unique among all human states of consciousness because its core nature is to hide, from other's detection as well as from our conscious awareness. Hence, a superficial concept of shame on a purely cognitive level will lift the lid off shame only momentarily, but lead to little permanent personal change. Therefore, unlike any other topic about human existence, shame demands a special methodology to attain the goal of human education and social wellbeing—a carefully constructed sequence of steps, such as I have planned in this book.

*

My vision, which transcends writing this book, is to create social change.

The convergent forces of technology and population growth have propelled social change onto an exponential curve of unbelievable acceleration in just the past one hundred years.

Although we have had the same basic *psychoemotional and biological structure* for two hundred thousand years, we are only very slowly learning about our intrinsic human nature. The existence of the shame response, or the fact that shame is a critical, primary human emotion, are recent discoveries, indeed.

In my book, "Hide and Play Dead," I subtly pointed out that neo-slavery has been instituted in America on a mass scale. This tragic situation is due to the consolidation of power among the higher echelons of a new ruling class, largely comprised of a corporate elite, and was preceded by century's old enslavement of workers in Third World countries. In "Overcoming Oppression," I further address this crisis and teach the reader how to effectively *recognize* and *resist* abuse and social oppression, as well as disclose the strategies of the corporate world that have been devised to keep us all enslaved.

Social oppression starts with shame induction during one's early developmental years, and escalates dramatically in the early 20s age group—the time just before most people enter the workforce. The beneficiaries of this oppression are a tiny fraction of the population that is mostly comprised of international corporate moguls and a

6

hereditary elite who have become the virtual rulers of the rest of humanity. The consolidation of both wealth and power in their hands has effectively diminished the middle class and pushed once thriving and self-sufficient masses into powerlessness, including joblessness or blatant exploitation in the workplace.

Reactionary political events have forged a countervailing movement; there has emerged a new and apparently massive force, formed in resistance to the status quo, which is ripe for the information presented in this book. We are witnessing a rapidly swelling tidal wave of concerned awareness about social oppression and the rise of corporate hegemony over the world population. The ever more conspicuous widening schism of wealth, wars based on financial exploitation, loss of trust in our financial institutions, political zealotry, blatant racial bigotry, and widespread corporate corruption and chicanery, have triggered a political backlash in the form of a snowballing succession of resistance movements.

The protest began with fringe activists such as the "Occupy Wall Street" group, or the "99% movement," and then mushroomed to a mainstream coalition of racial minorities, women, and young voters sufficient to re-elect President Obama. This was a momentous turning point in history, where a massive block of previously non-voting electorate had suddenly taken their first step towards self-empowerment.

The next stage of resistance to the status quo was perhaps a *backwards* protest— billionaire businessman Donald Trump became president riding on a powerful populist message: "Down with politics as usual!" But the blatant self-interest and undemocratic policies of the new administration ignited yet *another* wave of resistance both nationwide and internationally.

Now is the propitious moment to give these disgruntled masses, probably most Americans, full awareness of the nature of social oppression and the tools to resist it. This book will fit perfectly with their mindset: to *reframe* labor abuse, economic disparity and dwindling autonomy as widespread neo-slavery, is tantamount to giving a unifying slogan and a banner to the avengers of social injustice and financial inequality. It is a benign cover that draws attention, but not attack, from most Americans.

7

The newly emerged resistance is no longer content to feel stifled and diminished under the shame-based cloak of invisibility, the mantel of poverty or *relative* scarcity compared to the ultra-wealthy, to be eclipsed by partisan politics funded by the ruling elite, to toil under ruthless bosses for indecent wages, to give up creative autonomy in academic research and produce only the products funded by corporate strategists, to relinquish hopes for a better future or a secure retirement, or to die as soldiers fighting for the special interests of capitalist exploiters of the Third World.

Having grasped the straws of political power for the first time in their lives, many feel inspired to push harder and carry the cause for social equity with an unstoppable momentum. I believe that we are witnessing the grassroots beginning of a subtle social revolution, which will only intensify and escalate until true democracy is restored to the nation.

*

Shame, Technology, and Politics

Fifty years passed from the discovery of the concept of "stress" before the average American could understand and accept it without embarrassment or denial. From "shell shock" in the trenches of World War I, to the point that people now *boast* about how much stress they have, took many decades of education and social engineering.

I posit that ninety percent of our current stress is due to what you will learn to detect as "socially induced toxic shame," and I envision a day when shame will be as widely acknowledged and visible as "stress" has become. The greater the number of individuals who understand how to reverse the biosocial roots of shame, means a greater number of persons who can effectively resist abuse, heal from trauma, and confront the neoslavery imposed upon us by a relatively new and multi-national corporate and financial elite.

Technology, and especially *biotechnology*, is not popular among political activists or social engineers.

The misuse of technology by ruthless tyrants or unethical researchers has overshadowed the belief that technology could also

8

lead to a better human condition and an auspicious future for civilization. In the first half of the 20th century, medical and scientific breakthroughs were applauded by educated persons in affluent cultures— where the benefits of such advances were eclipsed be the larger social context of non-unionized labor in factories, and the ostentatious wealth of an elite class reminiscent of *The Great Gatsby.*

Since the advent of modern warfare— epitomized as much by nuclear, chemical and biological weapons production, as by fascist propaganda, torture of political dissidents, and commercial manipulation of mass consciousness—the tide of liberalism turned away from an optimistic stance towards technology; an innuendo of distrust and fear began to surround the topic of benevolent technological progress. The use of brain-altering biotechnologies fell into further opprobrium with the scandalous misuse of electro-convulsive shock therapy and frontal lobotomies in mental health institutions.

If most political and social scientists were to freely associate words related to "technology," I am convinced that they would list a very unsavory string. It is easy to reason that, if the causes of malaise and cruelty are based in our *socio-political culture*, then the cure for such problems must be found in large-scale *socio-political change.* Unfortunately, as I mentioned earlier, the path to progressive change is terribly slow and erratic, it is rife with regressive swings, and its momentum can be instantly halted by the creation of a mass disaster in any sector— whether imagined, contrived or real.

But I fully endorse and support the historical methodology of social engineering, provided it is non-violent.

I recently noticed a statement from a Democratic party activist:

Doug Jones has won Alabama's special Senate election and is headed to Washington to become the state's next U.S. Senator. This is a victory for hardworking Alabama families and for Democrats nationwide.

> Hundreds of thousands of supporters from all over the country rallied to make phone calls, send text messages, share social media posts, and donate whatever they could to help Doug get out the vote today. And we got the job done. Together.
>
> We've proven all year long that we can win anywhere when we *invest* in our state parties, *mobilize* the grassroots, and employ all our best practices, tools, and *technologies* to help our candidates win.
>
> —*Tom Perez, Democrats.org*

*

But what if there were breakthroughs creating synergistic, progressive social change technologies, that could also help cure hundreds of chronic, disabling and otherwise untreatable medical and psychiatric conditions?

What if some of these conditions were the cornerstone of reactionary and prejudicial ideologies, or the mindset of members of the conservative and self-serving corporate elite?

What if the technologies were the social activist's dream, for him or herself, as well as well as for building a massive, non-violent grassroots resistance movement?

Part Two: The Biological Basis of Oppression

Exactly, how does oppression work?
The answer might *surprise* you.

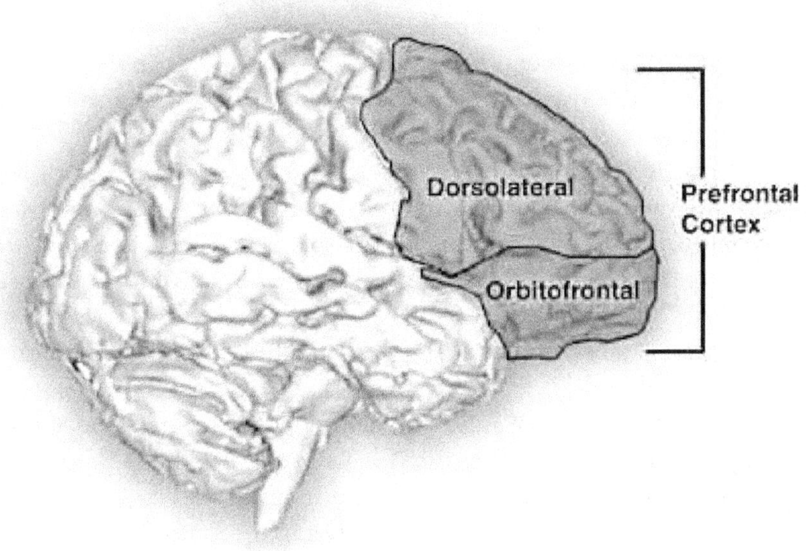

*

Part Two of this work discusses neuroscience research that describes how social oppression is coming to be viewed as an almost universal, socially-induced neurological imbalance.

*

THE PREFRONTAL SYNDROME

Something astonishing and unprecedented occurs in human development in the early 20s.

11

Technology for Social Reform

The exuberant idealism and grandiose expectations of the angry adolescent succumb to the sobering social realities of responsibilities, workloads, and debts. In many ways, the young adult is forced into submission by tremendous social pressure— and almost all do surrender.

At some time during this age span, an utter surrender to conformity, a psychological dismemberment of vital aspects of one's unique attributes, and a dampening of one's exploratory drive all seem to occur simultaneously for most persons.

The multifaceted diamond of one's potential is chiseled into a square peg. Passion recedes along with one's vision and dreams, which are either squashed or on permanent hold— to get to someday later, perhaps upon retirement, perhaps never.

The early 20's represents a very delicate time for human development and the loss of Self may manifest as psychopathology— an emotional problem. Clinical depression, adult attention-deficit disorders, bipolar illness, the first episodes of psychosis, and, most remarkably, clusters of personality disorders with extremely deep shame-based identity structures, appear in disproportionately large and growing numbers.

Something indeed strange has happened to human consciousness during this phase of final identity formation. All signs seem to point to a specific vulnerable part of the maturing human brain.

What has happened to the once liberated teenager? Why have his or her essential qualities succumbed to fixed social roles and a probable shame-based identity? How does trauma produce patterns of behavior that tend to repeat?

There is emerging evidence that stress and shame induction timed for the early 20's targets the most vulnerable, and last, window of human neurobiological development, and may deform the natural balance of the most evolved part of the brain. Moreover, thanks to anatomical studies, the precise locus of both guilt and shame is in the prefrontal cortex.

An interesting process has occurred at the same time as the constriction of one's identity structure is mandated by the prevailing social structure. The two, pea-sized prefrontal lobes of the brain reach **full maturation** in the early 20's. Anatomically, they are *equal* in size,

12

and they should theoretically be *equal* in contribution to human behavior.

*

The **<u>left prefrontal lobe</u>** leads to "approach" behavior— curiosity, exploration, inventiveness, originality, and creativity. It provides mental flexibility and spontaneity as well as sexual interest and experimentation with sexuality. It allows one to change a personality or identity structure, and to establish new patterns of behavior.

In sharp contrast, the **<u>right prefrontal lobe</u>** leads to "withdrawal" behavior— it inhibits the exploratory drive with an ability to suppress urges that could lead to socially unacceptable outcomes. Negative attitudes are strongly associated with right frontal love activity. It creates worry about the future consequences of stepping out of line and has the power to delay gratification— hoping and planning for a better or more rewarding result later.

The right prefrontal lobe blocks emotional signals, and fixes and maintains one's personality and actions into set patterns of activity. Simultaneously, it blocks new inputs, thoughts, and actions that are initially weakly established. Whenever a person tries to change— during a human change process— the right prefrontal lobe literally sabotages the new possibility by diverting attention to further re-enforcing already existing patterns instead.

It also forces conformity and obedience to established social processes: from obtaining permission to do something, to taking leadership or collaborating on a project. It maintains codified rules and moral, ethical, legal, and folk beliefs. It also maintains inflexible stereotypes that can influence behavior, often outside an individual's awareness.

A shame-based identity structure and all shame-based defenses are nearly perfectly described with anatomical precision. Indeed, all the aspects of toxic shame that I have described in "Overcoming Oppression," or that I will describe in upcoming writing, would appear to be corroborated by scientific research that pinpoints a locus of shame in the prefrontal lobes of the human brain.

*

Even more significantly, the right prefrontal lobe is especially designed to store certain themes in long-term memory; these themes have a strong emotional charge derived from the brain's limbic system. Such themes are unrelated to action plans or tasks to do. They represent stuck patterns of non-productive behavior.

It would appear likely that the themes that are stored in the right prefrontal lobe of the brain represent *old traumatic memories*— and that these themes are neurologically bound to repeat as well-maintained sets of maladaptive behavioral patterns.

In the context of "Overcoming Oppression," I am forced to conjecture that most of these memories involve episodes of toxic shame induction, including post-traumatic stress disorder (PTSD). Old traumas are thus neurologically wired to replay over and over. Dysfunctional early parental or peer bonding— or a history of abuse— repeats in choices of partners or work environments.

Whenever we try to change to healthier new patterns and choices, a tiny piece of brain tissue is wired to doubly reinforce our old patterns and choices! We are compelled to re-make bad choices that inevitably lead to self-sabotage and replicate the trauma.

The revelation is of utmost significance and deserves to be highlighted: A predominant shame-based identity appears to be literally branded into the neurologically-altered brain of an individual, along with deeply entrenched shame-based behaviors.

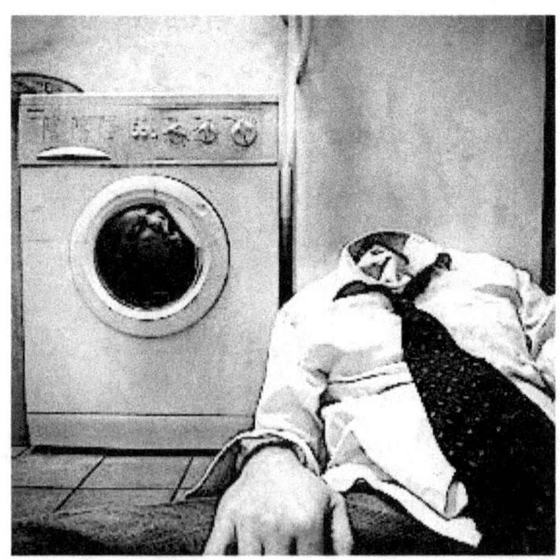

14

*

Hence, almost all of one's identity and its associated patterns of thoughts and behaviors are fixed by about age twenty-one to twenty-five— a time that coincides with the final maturation of biologically ingrained neuroanatomy. As virtually the entire field of psychology has known for decades, human neurosis is also pretty much set by this time.

Psychotherapy primarily addresses the early years as the root of the "problem state," and, therefore, the focus of the healing process. Whatever follows age twenty-one or so is just a repetition on the theme with a few minor changes. If anyone wants to know his or her issues, there is little need to look at recent triggering events unless there has been some devastating trauma.

Consequently, if one wants to know "how to heal," especially from shame and trauma, focus on re-molding or re-imprinting the developmental sequences up to the age of the early 20's— and the rest is usually a piece of cake.

I hypothesize that the timing of escalated social indoctrination leading into the labor force in the early 20's years is **NOT** by accident. A window of tremendous vulnerability in the maturation of the prefrontal lobes allows the conditioning to take nearly permanent hold on the entire finished identity of future workers.

Well-timed and sufficiently powerful, the brain will be stamped with right prefrontal lobe dominance; patterns of work tasks are imprinted along with fixed obedience to social processes and delayed gratification.

*

The toll that this neurobiological imprinting takes on human creativity and individuality is incalculable— and the benefits of creating a mass workforce physiologically altered to increase industrial productivity are questionable at this critical juncture of human history and planetary survival.

15

In this treatise, I am suggesting that social imprinting should strive for a *balance* in prefrontal contributions. Excessive activity of the left prefrontal lobe could lead to carefree risk-taking for immediate gratification and without regard for long-term consequences. If not carefully performed, or without the sophisticated use of alternate technologies, left lobe stimulation could also cause an attention-deficit type of distraction— leading to failure to orchestrate complex projects— as well as social deviance and mismanagement of anger.

Although the volume of neuropsychological and neuroanatomical research about the prefrontal lobes has exponentially increased over the past decade, they remain a vastly mysterious and complex part of the human brain and ongoing research is needed. Yet, currently, the entire shame response— along with guilt and remorse, trauma and PTSD, emotional inhibition and explosive rage, and depression or anxiety— appears related to prefrontal imbalance or asymmetry.

Furthermore, the liberating left prefrontal lobe is apparently *ten-fold more sensitive to stress* than the right; hence, the anxiety-driven and shame-based world that we inhabit, amplified by the media and sociopolitical uncertainty, may lead to irreversible damage—an ominous and intentional barrier to liberation from oppression. Fortunately, the therapy system espoused in "Overcoming Oppression" is clinically designed to correct the prefrontal imbalance, and new treatment trials continue to explore several biotechnologies that I will discuss in Part Four of this paper, "An Alternate Future."

Technology for Social Reform

The innovative qualities of ideas, possibilities and love are stamped into itemized quantities related strictly to the production of products, facts and services. It seems that the narrowest definition of functional roles is indoctrinated at the critical point of neurobiological maturation:

- Theorists become statistical researchers,
- Healers become mechanistic doctors,
- Entrepreneurs become MBA's,
- Visionaries become functionaries,
- Educators become lecturers or classroom disciplinarians,
- Statesmen and women become politicians and lawyers, and
- Studies in cooperative leadership are replaced with training for upper management.

Models of fixed behaviors, values and styles are thus rolled off the human assembly line with their brains anatomically stamped for the specific patterns, including ethics and personality features, designed for the job. Androids and artificial intelligences roll off another assembly line, with exponentially rising production and displacement of human workers, since they are *totally* programmable.

When business environments change, a *new* caveat is issued from the uppermost echelons of social privilege and a different human or mechanical model is drafted, while the *older* models are rendered obsolete and— in a narcissistic culture— discarded.

*

Clearly, the sociopolitical crisis that we collectively face has *other* roots, as I have explored in my books. Shame induction as part of our childrearing practices begins well before the first year of age. Educational systems exert tremendous pressure to mold the developing mind— forcing sequential stages of limited thought or cognition.

Personalities evolve largely by emulating role models found in our age-compatible peers and authority figures. Only a few lucky persons are spared the cerebral programming, largely because of unusual developmental experiences or very high intelligence.

The most damaging aberrance does seem to be rooted in the Prefrontal Syndrome, which is a new diagnostic label in neuropsychiatry. Of course, the measured imbalance between the prefrontal lobes, as determined by PET scans with EEG studies, varies greatly among individuals— as does the degree of constriction of one's free will and autonomy.

A further complexity, reiterating the goal of striving for prefrontal balance, is that a small percentage of the population will show excessive *left* prefrontal lobe activity— which is equally ominous and would seem to accompany anti-social or criminal behavior. The key is in making an accurate measurement of the relative activity of the two prefrontal regions, and then selecting biotechnological treatments and psychotherapeutic interventions accordingly.

Part Three: Our Imperiled Future

What is the global impact of prefrontal oppression? The answer might *shock* you.

*

Part Three of this series summarizes the grave sociopolitical implications of the prefrontal syndrome—a pervasive form of socially-induced brain impairment— for humanity and our planet.

*

It is startling that American childrearing practices and educational systems rely heavily on shame-induction, producing an easily conditioned mass of traumatized adults and passive workers. After reaching the age of the early twenties, almost all Americans succumb to regimented, oppressive structures of social control or become

19

incarcerated in our massive criminal justice system—which I refer to as "placing the mind cap."

There is no haven for the young adult today.

Most are too poor to live independently from their parents and enjoy the liberty of private housing, transportation, and material comforts—unless they submit to very oppressive institutions during the critical window of vulnerability in brain maturation. That might mean joining the military, entry into the lowest ranks of a corporate pyramid, the brutal indoctrination of a professional school, opting out for a seminary or religious cult, menial labor far beneath their potential, or existing homeless and on skid row.

If they try to prevail, they will accrue hefty debts far too early in life to pay off before crumbling under their weight of accrued interest. A few lucky ones may find a niche in Silicon Valley—only to be replaced by the next eager generation of programmers. In the ghettoes, some may find opportunity in crime, sports, or entertainment, but only a fraction will succeed and stay out of trouble. Social service is now a synonym for eternal poverty and ruthless superiors vying for limited grants.

Meanwhile, most citizens still imbue the very rich with awe and respect, and they are rarely the recipients of social stigma and scorn; instead, they have become icons and role models for most average people who bank on the Lotto for salvation. The values of acquisition and abundance have eclipsed the values of gratitude and generosity— or even harsher: *cruelty* has become acceptable, and *altruism* has become unpopular.

Among our less educated and poorer social groups, the immense and widespread popularity of narcissistic behavior is often termed "having an attitude." Such arrogant and selfish mores are precise replicas of the behavior of our ruling elite.

*

Conversely, for the historical poor, extreme humility, and even humiliation, were employed to force serfs and slaves to work incessantly, like criminals in chain gangs, in search of redemption. The builders of pyramids, grand cathedrals and palaces labored in *fear* of

20

their masters as much as in *awe* of their majestic production. Similarly, soldiers willing to die on a Crusade, pirates pillaging for treasures to bring back to a monarch, or palace guards prepared to defend the royals at all costs— *ALL* were all willing to postpone payment and contentment until the afterlife.

One of our most pervasive and prevailing beliefs is that one cannot get his or her needs met—at least without resorting to ploys to *force* others to grant them. This often means that the only power among the socially powerless is to manipulate others into *losing control,* and then just barely get vicarious and limited substitutes for our needs and wants.

It is not unlike the ignored child who must act up to get a parental reaction, which usually means punishment as a token for loving attention. Likewise, there is often a sadomasochistic element involved in violent protests, with an unconscious agenda to act out before imaginary "parents" to force them to pay attention… And the result is again often at the cost of punishment.

A healthy belief must be reinserted: **"I can *ASK* for what I want, and I can *GET* what I need in life!"** A major part of finding contentment is to be direct in our communications and negotiate for what we want— and *sometimes* we will get it.

The core of our collective human survival is the premise that everyone can get what they need— including love— and it should generally be readily granted. If it is *not,* perhaps a social revolution or other more aggressive intervention is mandated to redress the injustice or to improve the performance of our institutions. Yet, in such circumstances, which are becoming rampant, one may not have to storm the Bastille to get our needs met; negotiation and compromise play a major role.

*

The schism of wealth has birthed a three-headed dragon of insatiable greed for wealth and power.

The disparity will, among other things, lead to an economic collapse *far* worse than the Great Depression; economists anticipate a record-breaking crisis due to a drop in the demand for goods as the world's population becomes too impoverished to consume them. The loss of the purchasing power of the marginated *middle-upper class,* down through the nearly extinct *middle class,* may topple production.

And, as in any global catastrophe, the weakest—*or the poorest*—of the human population will perish. Only the richest will survive and quite probably, as a replay of the staged economic recession of 2007, the rich will become considerably richer and more powerful.

The situation is like the infectious plagues that beset Eurasia during most of the medieval centuries, which wiped out the entire European, and much of the Asian, population— sparing *only* the aristocracy, which isolated themselves in their rural sanctuaries and castles. A largely unknown historical fact is that the current population of the continent is comprised almost solely of descendants of this historical ruling class. Perhaps the best analogy for the schism of wealth, then, is an infectious plague capable of exterminating most of humanity, and leaving only the rulers prosperous and well.

The crime of economic genocide goes unnoticed. But the effacement of the world's poorest three and a half billion inhabitants will be a scourge that will tarnish the conscience of historians and journalists, who dare to reveal the atrocity in graphic records and photographs. The foundation of a civilization based on democratic ethics can crumble in wars merely carried out by paper transfers of wealth, from the *poor*— including the professional, academic, and entrepreneurial sectors— to the *rich*.

The three and a half billion poor inhabitants of most of the Second World and below will simply vanish by starvation and the physical diseases of poverty. The intentional genocide of half of the global population is regarded by some as a neat design to permanently concentrate money and power in the hands of the few. It simultaneously serves to resolve overpopulation by eliminating the unlucky underclass—a group perceived as a burden requiring welfare as the expense of the rich, as parasites deserving extermination, or as non-participants in a capitalist economy.

*

22

Technology for Social Reform

The myth of worldwide overpopulation has been dispelled and replaced with the ethical and reasonable goal of limiting *further* population growth. Still, the stated objective of outspoken members of the elite is quite specific: to reduce the world population to one-fifth its current size. The impending massive economic collapse and environmental restructuring will achieve that with precision.

But the only way to ethically curb over-population is to *first* redistribute wealth equitably, such that the poor do not need offspring as their only retirement security in old age, and then, *secondly*, to provide quality healthcare and education, which reduces infant mortality and gives a meaning to life beyond mere reproduction.

If the sixty-six richest individuals in the world were to philanthropically donate just *half* of their wealth to humanity, poverty would be eradicated *double*. The largesse could also provide ample and universal healthcare, and give the best education to every student on Earth. As of last count, only six of these ultra-wealthy persons says he or she might *consider* sharing their legendary fortunes.

If the elite continues its narcissistic path, invading all our fundamental social institutions and propelling us into a two-class society, we—and our planet—are doomed to regress to a feudal state reminiscent of the Dark Ages. All the warning signs are present— *and*, as I have pointed out, the ruling class is now equipped with far more advanced technologies to manipulate and oppress the human brain.

23

*

Even more startling and tremendously relevant is the reinstitution of slavery in America.

Neoslavery is as *conspicuous* as the elimination of our former middle class, which is now a generic working class. And the impending extinction of the working class is already obvious; especially work groups whose unionization has been a prime pet peeve for the elite for over a century and a half. Workers will survive under ruthless oppression as the "new lower class," along with equally subjugated skilled laborers from the industrial sector and millions of mercenary soldiers.

Lumped together, as during the height of the Roman Empire and throughout the medieval era, the emerging working class will be stifled like *serfs* of the "new Dark Ages."

Neoslavery is as *subtle* as the suppression and demotion of the bourgeoisie and intelligentsia—both of which are now controlled under the cloaked tend protected vestments of multinational corporate entities. Social change or social revolution cannot be achieved without the leadership of these two divested groups.

24

The demotion of our most educated classes to abject powerlessness and total dependency on the elite replicates the static *guilds and artisans* of the medieval era.

Thus, the two equally disempowered, and originally quite discrete, social classes or groupings—the former middle class and the bourgeoisie— will be in the *same* boat, and may be destined to become a united coalition.

There is a mood of cynical despair that subtly pervades almost all American social strata— which are *all* on the verge of extinction, elimination, and perhaps banishment... As the fringe at the supreme top of the social ladder, the social elite, squeezes the population into ever-greater debt and servitude. A "revolt of rising expectations" — like the French Revolution— occurs when the bourgeoisie is frustrated and has higher expectations than their real level of compensation. A mob of angry masses invariably follows, and then a violent insurrection erupts.

Especially in America and Europe, the former middle class and the educated bourgeoisie will not disappear easily. The human population, at least in the First World democracies of North America and Western Europe, will not tolerate social or economic oppression beyond a critical point of suffering.

To reenact a conquest of the elite's last potential markets and adversaries by confiscation of their artificially devalued assets —

25

holdings that can be instantly and secretly swept away at pennies on the dollar— would be thoughtless and foolish. Although the elite can do this by a massive transfer of capital, and with the mere touch of an **economic button**, the consequences would be grave.

The ripple effects of such larceny may well lead to a disastrous long-term backlash. It is not possible to simply vanquish the gifted minds and staunch workers of First World nations.

A violent and armed revolution against the elite has been forecast by many political scientists, think-tank sociologists, policy analysts, and international watchdog agencies— and the result of a mass uprising is *not thinkable*. It is probable that the ruling elite, which controls the economy, owns all our natural resources, and oversees the military-industrial complex, would— with the narcissistic tendencies of its leadership—brutally suppress an armed revolt.

The crushed protest would then evolve into an underground resistance army…

Factions would probably destroy any unified ideology…

And, eventually, a **nuclear button** would likely be pressed by one side, or one faction, or another…

*

The fundamental requirement for relationships is a mutual quest for stable bonding based on love— and the capacity to love is *inversely* related to the presence of shame. Hence, all shame-based persons have a major disruption in interpersonal intimacy—they are incapable of true love or self-love.

Less love equals more shame… And more shame equals more people with a personality disorder—of which Narcissism is the most common.

We are faced with something that is perhaps worse than financial collapse— We have a crippling burden of shame in seventy million Americans who have at least one personality disorder.

I believe, as do most mental health experts, that the prevalence of all shame-based disorders is rising, and until desensitization for shame is widespread, we will be plagued with an ever-increasing prevalence

26

of personality disorders—along with the consequent traumatization and burnout of their victims.

In many respects, certain personality disorder types are the bane of social function, as well as representing the leaders of our society. That is because the most aggressive forms of this disorder tend to rise to preeminence in social rank— thus, the wall of vested power represents a blockade against *both* interpersonal love and progressive change within our society.

Hatred and cruelty accompany a reactionary personality.

Such people consider their mental illness a blessing, largely because they have no qualms about exploiting, looting, or inflicting toxic shame on other people. Moreover, being *different* suggests to many of them being *unique*— or superior to ordinary folk who have the weakness of needing love.

Let's recap:

- American childrearing practices and educational systems still rely on shame induction.
- After the early 20s, the prefrontal syndrome seals the fate of almost all persons.
- The young succumb easily to oppressive structures of social regimentation.

- Most citizens imbue the very rich with awe and respect, and wish to emulate them.
- The prevailing belief is that one cannot get his or her needs met without force.
- Hence, cruelty has become acceptable, and altruism has become unpopular.

- Economists anticipate a record-breaking crisis due to the schism of wealth.
- A world war carried out by paper transfers from the poor to the rich is inevitable.
- The weakest—*or the poorest*—of the human population will perish in economic genocide.

27

- The foundation of a civilization based on humane ethics is crumbling.
- We are being propelled into a two-class society, reminiscent of a feudal state.
- The ruling class is equipped with advanced technologies to oppress the human brain.

- The elite continues to invade all our fundamental social institutions, especially government.
- The reinstitution of slavery includes the suppression of the bourgeoisie and intelligentsia.
- Social revolution cannot be achieved without the leadership of these two groups.

- A revolt occurs when the bourgeoisie has unmet expectations.
- A mob of angry masses invariably follows the bourgeoisie.
- The result of a mass uprising is not thinkable.

- Factions would destroy any unifying structure or ideology.
- The crushed protest would evolve into an underground resistance.
- Eventually, the nuclear button would likely be pressed by one side or faction.

- All personality disorders are on the rise.
- Loveless malignant Narcissism is the most common personality disorder.
- Less love equals more shame; more shame equals more people with a personality disorder.

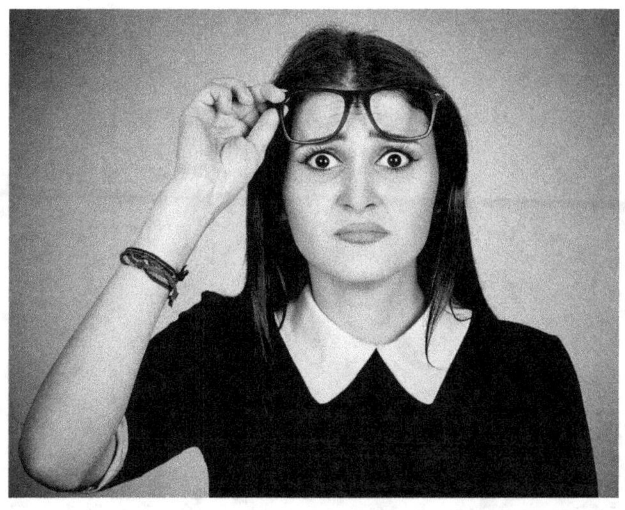

WHAT ON EARTH CAN WE DO TO AVERT DISASTER?

Most humans are still operating from the emotional midbrain and from the reptilian brainstem— with little empathy, an aggressive drive for competitive dominance over other humans, and a crude sexual instinct. The amygdala adds the only true emotion, *rage*, which is an unrestrained variant of anger.

Are these not the qualities that membership among the narcissistic, ruling elite requires?

Very, very few humans have transitioned to the executive functions of the prefrontal lobes, which are the most evolved part of the human brain that no other species possesses. Unfortunately, socially induced derangement of this region is now almost universal, resulting is an easily oppressed mass of laborers and virtual slaves.

If there *were* an evolved empath, someone who had retained a balanced and reasonably intact set of left and right prefrontal lobes, he or she would almost represent a new *subspecies* of Homo sapiens. But the social climate would be hostile to any *single* human who might evolve to such a level. As most predators, the ruling elite would show a merciless narcissistic tendency to exploit, destroy, and then discard the rare being.

29

But a *large group* of evolving persons could perhaps survive…

30

Part Four: An Alternate Future

**How can we reverse social oppression?
The answer may *motivate* you.**

*

Part Four of this series reveals converging *psychobiological* ways to reverse the prefrontal syndrome; if utilized, these treatments can indirectly lead to a spontaneous mass resistance movement to redress *sociopolitical* oppression.

*

31

CULTURAL ROOTS

Fortunately, there are many ways to achieve liberation from oppression and resist the molds of the emerging creators of mass consciousness. First, as we return to our personal, cultural, and spiritual roots, we quickly become much more powerful than an isolated individual who is cut off from the sense of having a place in history. The initial stage of slavery has always been based on the displacement of the slave from his or her ancestral legacy as well as the extended family and village culture that preserves those roots.

When evening comes, I enter the courts of the ancients, and am welcomed by them. There I taste the food that alone is mine, and for which I was born. And there I make bold to speak to them and ask the motives of their actions, and they, in their humanity, reply to me. And for the space of hours I forget the world, remember no vexation, fear poverty no more, tremble no more at death—I pass indeed into their world. —*Excerpted from the Literary Works of Machiavelli, trans. J.R. Hale. (Oxford: 1961)*

It is vital to reconnect with *both* one's genetic past and environmental history, with *all* our formative roots, to understand our current dilemmas, problems, and issues— as well as to recognize our innate resources, gifts and potential. In "Hide and Play Dead," I united the two strands by closely examining in tandem both my genetic or ancestral legacy and my environmental or lifetime socialization.

Genealogy is a largely ignored missing tool for social change. It can link *genetic predispositions* with *developmental history*. But, to be a liberating and motivating method for intrapsychic and social change, it must be sufficiently detailed— with information about the lives and aspirations of our ancestors, as well as the trans-generational transmission of childrearing practices. It must be much more than a mere genealogical chart revealing only names, lineages, and perhaps places.

History does repeat itself, and a wise social engineer must see the big picture—especially about the enduring nature of slavery. Moreover, the experiences of our ancestors, including their beliefs, struggles, and life's lessons, form much of the basis for a congruent individual identity.

This big picture about our roots must become fully conscious before effective action can be taken, lessons re-learned, mistakes avoided, and behaviors re-imprinted—ultimately leading to freedom from oppression and to healthy individuation.

Genetic research is rapidly advancing and will *someday* offer insight into our entire psychobiological nature. It was of utmost value in the discovery of many details about my own forbearers. But the subtle mysteries of individual human nature—including both adaptive and problematic behaviors— are *currently* best discerned by a thorough examination of one's genealogy and autobiographical history.

This was the case with my maternal lineage, for which published autobiographies, historical research, and transgenerational storytelling explained the origins of my genetic identity with precision—back to 300 years into the past.

If the genealogical charts and stories of our ancestors—in many cases, including one's parents—are unavailable, unknown or lost, then inexpensive genetic analysis, such as from "23andMe.com," sheds light on our racial or ethnic roots. It may even open a door to

33

communicating with lost relatives who may know about the circumstances of our forbearers.

This was the case with my orphaned father, who had no idea that he was half-Jewish; luck provided him with his original birth certificates, where the parents' names had not been crossed out, by mere oversight or accident; the full genealogical history then became transparent with a little additional research.

Full awareness of who we truly are, why we suffer, and how to become free requires detailed knowledge of our ancestry, which we must examine to discern repeated trans-generational patterns or themes. Moreover, our self-esteem depends upon having a sense of having a place in linear history.

Hence, a large part of my adventure of self-discovery evolved from researching the lessons of my ancestral roots, as well as my developmental history, which *together* helped form the core of my new identity.

For instance, I did not know, until long *after* starting to write about my personal experience of neoslavery and recognizing global neoslavery, that most of my maternal ancestors had been devoted to doing the same work for a span of over three hundred years. Only then did I embark *without hesitation* upon my current calling and work, for it became my preordained destiny.

Conversely, to lose knowledge of our ancestral *past*, or to be cut off from our genealogical roots, destroys the foundation of a population's history. Then, the masses become exclusively dependent upon *current*, and invariably toxic, social conditioning.

The consequent loss of self-esteem, self-efficacy and the disruption of one's psyche is tantamount to smashing the cohesion and sequencing of cellular chromosomes, themselves. Research has recently proved that ancient historical trauma is embedded in our genetic code, and may reside there for millennia. Hence, "once a slave, always a slave" …

Depression, chronic disease, and premature death manifest more readily in the victim who has lost his or her roots. The African American life expectancy remains ten to fifteen years shorter than the European descendants for this reason, among other factors. Such uprooted unfortunates are invariably among the most oppressed of all

34

persons, and they are rarely capable of becoming advocates for social change.

Most commonly, this tragedy involves the relocation of indigenous peoples to reservations or into slavery in foreign lands. A crushing, oppressive process is engendered when this literal uprooting is combined with repudiation of a culture's collective historical wisdom and suppression of their oral and written history.

*

LITERACY AND EDUCATION

Even worse than severing our historical roots, is to enforce *illiteracy*, such as the anti-literacy laws during the centuries of American slavery. When such strict laws were violated, they often carried a lethal punishment, equal or worse to that of runaway slaves. Without the written word, one's past has no documentation, and, when combined with *secrecy*, almost all transmission about one's ancestry and true kin is effectively blocked from our offspring.

35

In other words, the loss of invaluable historical messages leads to the loss of our truest identity and, I repeat, leaves us *completely vulnerable* to only a few, crafted templates of dysfunctional, shame-based, or oppressive identity structures. These identity molds are deftly imprinted by social sculptors—especially the ruling corporate elite. Slavery, neoslavery, or slave-related behaviors are easily imposed upon such a malleable consciousness.

I was again lucky… After a liberal arts education among the ruling class, I could not divest myself of an acquired instinct to be creative and think independently. Because of this, I knew that, eventually, I would break completely free of bondage. A grand education was the key to my freedom, but unfortunately, most Americans are unable to benefit from this expensive tool, which slowly, but deeply, digs a path up from the trenches of psychic oppression.

Both childrearing practices and formal education are major themes in "Overcoming Oppression," and the fork in the road between *oppressive submission* versus *creative autonomy* for young minds has never been more slanted to the former. I recommend that the reader look at the early chapters on child development and education in "Overcoming Oppression" to get a sense of the magnitude of the problem.

Uneducated masses, persons subjugated by doctrinaire training, and all those raised "by the rod," are rarely able to embrace or support positive social change.

They are terrified of change.

*

INTERPERSONAL LOVE

A capacity to truly offer romantic love to another, and the blessing of being able to receive unconditional love from another, are the two greatest assets needed in the struggle for the ultimate freedom from shame. Spiritual love produces nearly the same phenomenon, especially when one is connected to a broad support system through a religious group. The re-acquisition of the full human love response is

36

a central part of anti-oppression training, as I have laid out in detail in "Overcoming Oppression."

Evidence abounds that supports the pivotal role of love as our most powerful way to resist oppression, and to ultimately free us from toxic shame. I will leave a precise summary of shame desensitization and anti-oppression training for later, although I will touch on a few pieces of the process in the following section of this paper.

But for now, consider that:

Love is greater than existing psychotherapeutic techniques.
Love is greater than having the world's best liberal education.
Love is greater than any subjugating force in the world.
Love is greater than the combination of all these and more.

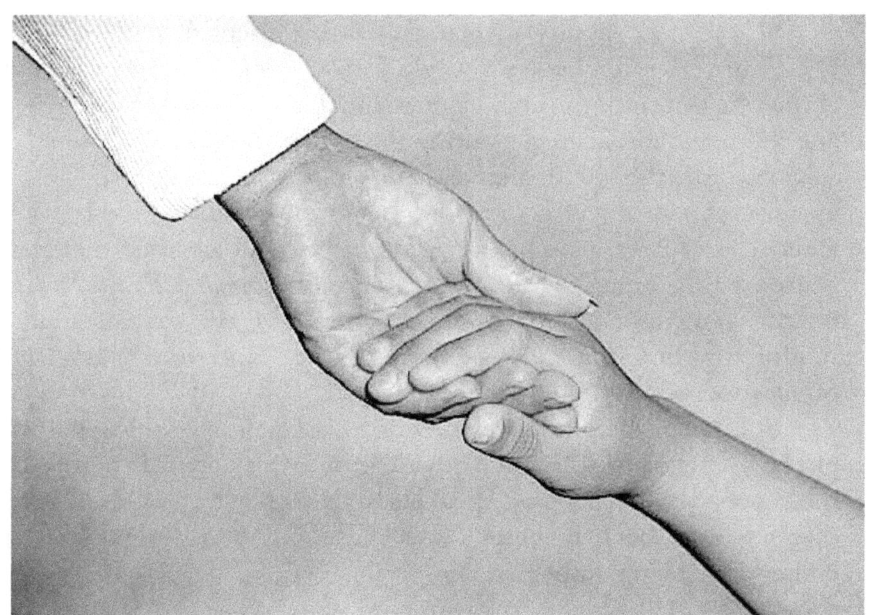

*

TECHNOLOGIES FOR SOCIAL REFORM

Sometimes, true science appears to be science fiction.

What if there existed a thrilling, albeit daunting, project to propel civilization and human evolution through a safe quantum leap of decades—well past the political and socioeconomic crisis looming over the globe?

I envision three phases of social change, using the technologies that I and others have either invented or utilized, to achieve a time warp across every sector of our bio-social existence.

*

Phase One is based on a unique writing technology.

The complex literary format that I first used in "Hide and Play Dead" has been dubbed: *The Trojan horse of literature*. I have assembled about one dozen of the core elements that are required to dramatically alter human neuroanatomy during the passive process of reading.

Some of the fundamentals are: *writer-reader transference*—or the creation of a strong affective bond between the author and his or her audience, *cadencing* —or the alternation of highly charged material or genres with calming or resolutional narratives, *multi-level construction*—or the transmission of the same messages on several mutually reinforcing conscious and subconscious levels, and *serialization*—or the publication of multiple, synergistic works.

But I must defer until later a *complete* explanation of this remarkably effective literary methodology, which, once mastered, is perhaps the most persuasive writing or speaking style to reach the public-at-large that has ever been invented. I will just give you a glimpse of the embedded literary strategies.

*

Here I describe literary transference, as used in "Hide and Play Dead."

38

THE CRUCIAL NEED TO KNOW THE WRITER
The Nature of Literary Transference

My highly unusual life history encompasses nearly all the major variations on the theme of shame, and serves as an excellent example of the book's focus. I am by nature the best "case history" I know for the topic. My "issues" also mirror many social issues of major current interest in American society. Thus, I am obligated to boldly take the risk of full self-disclosure to best exemplify the entire treatise on shame. But this alone will not attain the book's goals of healing the sedentary reader.

Although the book contains valuable intellectual and factual material, as well as technological sophistication, it would still fail to reach the goal of *durable change* in the reader if he or she cannot personally bond with me, the writer. The necessity of creating an intimate connection with the writer is nowhere more essential than when addressing the subject of shame.

Such a connection is arguably the most important tool required for a successful outcome in this book, on this subject, and perhaps, in educational and social change processes in general. Shame, abuse and trauma involve the rupture of significant interpersonal bonds, therefore the "cure" requires the re-establishment of human connectedness.

This is what I call "literary transference" (or "writer-reader transference"), which has been woefully under-utilized and—to my knowledge— rarely been attempted in nonfiction books rooted in social commentary or having an informative nature. By multiple invitations for the reader to enter my life and vicariously identify with me, I become a "real live person" with whom the reader then develops an intimate and personal link.

SEVERAL INNOVATIVE TECHNIQUES ARE USED TO ACCOMPLISH THIS FEAT:

1. I firmly and definitively step off the pedestal of professionalism and the

ladder of being an authority figure, thereby making myself *equal* to the reader. I create the sense that "we're in the same boat."

2. I fully *expose* myself as a vulnerable human being who is, in all basic ways, just like the reader. I build an emotional tie with the reader by such self-revealing openness.

3. To consolidate the rapport, I convince the reader that I am telling my truth, for a manipulative liar would never be so open and vulnerable; thus, I invoke the reader's *trust*.

4. I forge an initial bond to my early life, and only slowly to my adult life. Who cannot but love an innocent, bullied *child?*

5. I insert personal photographs, some quite revealing of my intimate life, at key points in the book. These are generally of my family and myself, as if showing a photo album to a friend.

6. I invite the reader into my current-time life and take the reader on the adventure of my own self-healing, showing genuine surprise as it mysteriously unfolds, as if he or she were a *fellow traveler.* We are both seriously wondering, "Well, what's going to happen next?"

7. I chronicle synchronistic events that happen during the process of writing with emotional zeal, and with cadenced stories designed to deepen and consolidate our bond and to *pace* the reader's own emotions.

8. I do not force the reader to change his or her beliefs or behaviors, or even to agree with the implicit social messages; therefore, I skirt around *resistance.*

9. I *humbly* relate the thrill and agony of being a first-time writer, as I employ the genre of "writing about the process of writing" and— of paramount significance, "how *writing* changes the writer," which is subliminally associated with "how *reading* changes the reader."

10. I make myself as an example of the exact shame desensitization process that I am implicitly teaching the reader. With transference sealed, the reader will believe: *"Well, if Michael can do it... So can I!"*

11. Ultimately, the reader will not just think and say to others, "I read a great book." He or she will be more inclined towards a much stronger word-of-mouth pitch, especially for an intended series: *"I really love this author!"*

"Cadencing" briefly explained:

40

> After any stressful or emotionally charged passage, I *immediately* proceed to urge the reader towards lower, more relaxed arousal levels. This may mean doing therapeutic somatic or other exercises in specific categories, or l relating a resolutional account of healthy shame and love. This way, I can safely lead the reader through a neurobiological re-imprinting process. The overall goal is to maximize healing by *extinguishing* the reader's sensitivity to shame, or *desensitizing* one's history of abuse and trauma during any stage of life.

"Multi-level construction" in a nutshell:

> The use of allegorical depictions of a fictional "Johnny" in most chapters prove helpful for many readers to identify with, and to "get" the essence of the book on a preconscious level. Dramatic personal memoirs and true life stories are designed to heighten both awareness and interest, as they are written in the genre of literary and poetic prose.
>
> The *main text* contains information, studies, and case histories—as is usual in books dealing with psychology; however, the expository or academic writing is kept to a minimum for a reason: **I do not want the reader to shift into excessive abstraction and ego defenses**. The clinical case histories and studies herein are chosen to have a poignant emotional impact on the reader, which feeds into the neuro-restructuring paradigm.
>
> The book is *holographic* and the same messages are repeated in many different, mutually reinforcing styles. I will also utilize multiple, parallel and mutually reinforcing levels of the brain's anatomical structure to convey the "message."
>
> The theoretical basis, the unique built-in process, is such that *however* the reader digests the book, his or her neurobiological imprints of trauma will be dramatically reduced, and the capacity for love in all its forms—especially compassion and altruism—will deepen.

Learning requires *repetition*—especially when the prefrontal syndrome has been established in the early 20s. As I mentioned earlier, the left prefrontal lobe routinely disrupts the establishment of new thoughts or behaviors, and shunts bio-electricity to deeply reinforce old patterns instead. For this reason, "serialization," or a series of books with different angles, styles, and topics are needed.

With two major works and four anthologies, my relatively new writing career is off to a good start; workbooks, children's books, professional guidebooks, and scores of essays and short story narratives are in the hopper.

"Serialization," under the series name of **Overcoming Social Oppression**:

My second, major book, "Overcoming Oppression" deepens the shame desensitization experience acquired by reading the first major book of the series, "Hide and Play Dead." This *second* book permits a deeper assimilation of the new neural pathways or neurosignatures initiated while reading my *first* book. A person who chooses to read *only* "Hide and Play Dead," or only "Overcoming Oppression," or *reverse* the order of reading the two books, will still be able to cope with the content and learn, heal and change for the better.

My series of four anthologies, which are shorter collections of narratives and occasional essays, focus on specific challenges one faces in an oppressive cultural context. These are the creation of a unique *racial, sexual, adult,* and *spiritual* identity—With literary transference, I pace and lead the reader *away from* shame and/or trauma, and *towards* a bold, shame-free Self.

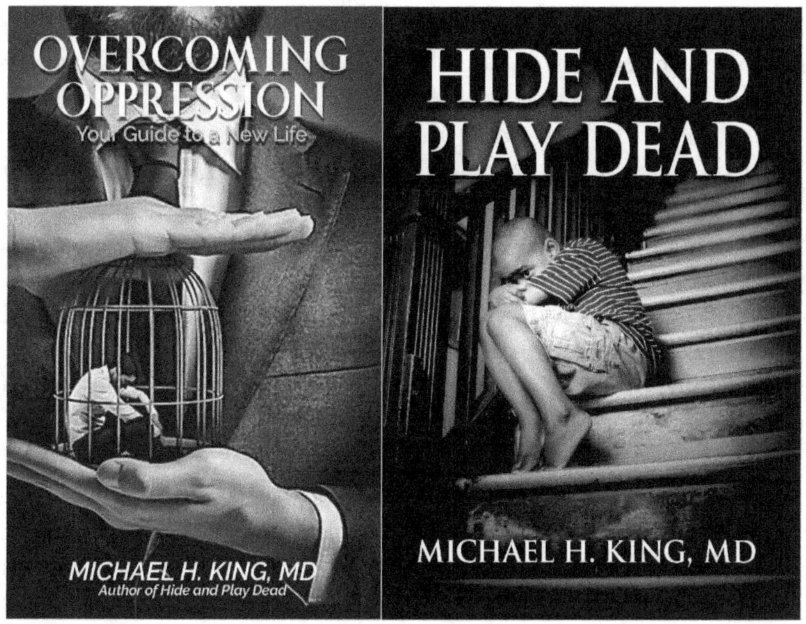

*

Phase Two is where conscious awareness of the precise nature of human oppression and a dead-on-the-mark process to repel it are widely disseminated.

To reiterate, oppression requires a ***cascade*** of human predation. This cascade starts with toxic shame induction beginning in childhood, and childrearing practices are currently based more in toxic shame induction than corporeal punishment. *Toxic shame* establishes the foundation of widespread abuse, most of which is generally unrecognized.

Interpersonal and socioeconomic abuse flourishes due to ignorance about human predatory behavior—especially solipsism, in which individuals become objects to be exploited for one's own gratification. When *abuse* is adequately intense, or when a critical surge in Narcissism overwhelms the ramparts of our social institutions, individual or mass *trauma* results.

43

A traumatized population is prone to *oppression*— enslaved by debt, intensified by collapsing social services. At this point, oppression is easily achieved with fixed neurobiological imprints and impairment.

The cascade from toxic shame, to abuse, to trauma, and to oppression is now neurologically ingrained in most persons. But the information in "Overcoming Oppression" dispels ignorance and disseminates conscious awareness of the precise nature of human oppression, and the therapeutic techniques learned by reading the book and doing the required exercises embedded within it, represent a well-tested and proven process to repel it.

The core of human suffering cannot easily manifest when my psychotherapeutic system is practiced.

There are many parts to the human change process that are both original and effective. The two most potent experiential lessons needed for most activists, and to shift from sociopolitical passivity to organized action in a divided populace are "Shame Desensitization Therapy" and "Anti-Oppression Training."

It would be impossible to succinctly summarize these modalities, for, I again emphasize, the lessons are learned by *immersion* into the nonfiction and self-help literature. This is ideally *augmented* by individual and group trainings or psychotherapy, and—if available—customized *biotechnological interventions.*

*

The cornerstone of <u>Shame Desensitization Therapy</u> is to learn to instantly recognize toxic shame in oneself, and to *consciously* reverse its most accessible effects. The physiological and psychological torment of toxic shame are the *same*, whether they are inflicted upon children or adults, or upon political prisoners or a young member of the ruling elite. Toxic shame is *deadly* for all organ systems including the most evolved parts of the human brain…

The easily learned, and quickly mastered, physiological shifts to block the initial stage of oppression involve a change in one's breathing pattern, muscle tone—especially the jaw, and awareness of one's skin sensation. To some degree, these are the foundation of all relaxation

44

techniques. But to detoxify shame, a modified and precise process must be acquired.

The cognitive shift, which involves learning dissociative techniques, essentially frees one of self-doubt, self-judgment, and self-sabotage—Or, really, the establishment of unwavering self-esteem *without* arrogance.

The immediate benefit of practicing the above is to remove oneself from being the target of social predators. The activist using these techniques also begins to gain a wide array of health benefits, including a sustainable high energy level that naturally combats burnout.

There is a myriad of *other* benefits, such as synchronization and instant rapport with any person, most of whom are likely to have a shame-based personality to some degree. The resulting simpatico prevents resistance and paves the way to dismantle another's ideological paranoia about social change.

*

<u>Anti-Oppression Training</u> flows naturally from a sequence of stepwise and stacked experiential lessons in self-help work or in interactive psychotherapy. The culminating skill confers immunity from brain-washing or propaganda, from isolation or corporate profiling, and from disadvantageous defenses that may lead to spiteful hatred or condescension when interacting with persons whose beliefs differ drastically from one's own.

I believe that the ultimate core of Anti-Oppression work involves the intentional *re-activation of the nearly extinct human love response*, and to achieve this goal is far simpler than one might imagine. Effective social activism is based on community building, bridge building, and non-violent communication.

We must bond with those whose beliefs seem to be the antithesis of our own, just as in negotiating a peace accord between warring parties in partisan vendettas across the globe.

Only by repeatedly re-evoking love, and being able to demonstrate the most powerful of all emotions in our visible physiognomy and physiology, can we block the cascade of toxic shame, abuse, trauma

45

and free ourselves and other individuals from susceptibility to social oppression.

Only by empathic caring can we transcend trivial differences, and open others' eyes to the over-arching and ultimate horror of modern life which we all share: *economic neoslavery.*

Phase Three is where biotechnology plays a major role.

When biotechnologies, which can reverse neurological imbalances caused by shame, are added to the equation, miracles can happen. Devices such as EEG biofeedback, trans-cranial direct electric current stimulation (tDCS) or magnetic interference— with PET scan and laser-guided precision— can spark creativity, as well as social approach and engagement behavior in oppressed persons.

Treatments are quick and effective. They're safe with no bad side-effects. They're non-invasive, non-surgical, and non-pharmaceutical. The devices are inexpensive, and most are now readily available— generally without requiring medical supervision.

The biotechnologies also appear capable of healing, or ameliorating, hundreds of chronic, disabling, and otherwise untreatable medical and psychiatric conditions—illnesses that afflict up to two-thirds of the American population. A random sampling these conditions includes

46

obesity, depression, chronic fatigue syndrome, and personality disorders—*especially* Narcissism and sociopathy.

What this means is that demand for the technology will be *driven by medical necessity,* with millions of desperate consumers who want to be well. A mass distribution to almost every household in America is not beyond realistic possibility.

*

The ripple effects of using these emerging technologies to treat the prefrontal region of the brain are dramatic.

I emphasize that all the techniques that I have developed and mentioned thus far *also* produce these predictable changes— as they all target the common root of the emotion of shame. But, as with many therapy-based change processes, the use of several synergistic interventions leads to a *logarithmic*, not additive, result.

Neuro-technological studies have amply demonstrated curious behavioral changes…

• Depression evaporates and a modest state of euphoria sets in. People begin to feel happy again.

• Narcissistic and sociopathic features begin to vanish as empathy flourishes. Quite literally, criminals change into conscientious citizens.

• Cruelty transforms into altruism, which initiates a renaissance of all forms of the once-lost love response.

• A quasi-adolescent level of energy, adaptability, ingenuity, and autonomy vanquishes despair, cynicism, self-doubt, and passivity.

• Certain psychic skills seem to emerge in some people, including precognition, telepathy, and clairvoyance.

• Ideological, stereotyped, or prejudicial divisions disappear— along with xenophobia and social phobias.

• Postponement of gratification stops, such that fulfillment of one's essential needs and rights changes into peaceful activism demanding equity.

• And, most significantly, what is called "non-specific approach and engage behavior" fuels human interconnectedness.

Technology for Social Reform

Again, I must leave the precise protocols and equipment designs for another arena and time. But I can personally attest to the impressive impact of using even the simplest trans-cranial direct current electrical stimulator, commonly available via the Internet at a very modest price (under $200, and as low as $60).

One of the most exciting prospects for the use of such devices is the treatment of personality disorders. As I have alluded to earlier, most members of our current corporate and social elite—the ultimate power-mongers with incalculable hidden wealth—tend to have a narcissistic personality disorder.

In "Overcoming Oppression," I discuss the ramifications of what experts consider to be a rapidly expanding epidemic of Narcissism throughout society, afflicting now up to twenty percent of the American population. There is no force more oppressive and dangerous than a "Little Napoleon," whose ruthless drive for money and power is insatiable.

If there indeed exists one adversarial character capable of destroying progressive change, a type of person bent on another cascade of *exploiting, destroying, and discarding* fellow humans, it would belong to the inchoate realms of Narcissism.

Most narcissists experience a paradoxical pleasure upon seeing the poor and homeless, as the plight of the unfortunate somehow confirms the narcissist's superiority. Although they are convinced of their God-given superiority, they are truly sick people who invariably lead a loveless life. If even a small percentage of such persons were to experiment with any of the technologies that I have mentioned, or new technologies on the horizon, our collective human condition might palpably improve.

Even more interesting to many is the proof that criminal behavior, or sociopathy, is yet another personality disorder that is treatable using magnetic interference of the prefrontal lobes. The implications of nullifying our criminal justice system as obsolete, and returning reformed convicts to our communities as conscientious neighbors, are *immense*.

Astute political scientists may realize that among the global trillionaires who are at the helm of *all* our vital institutions exist a shocking number of veteran psychopaths who entered the business

48

world, perhaps originally to feign a legitimate cover for their operations. Their recent acquisitions in the corporate sector were funded by inestimable cash reserves—gained from trafficking in drugs, weapons, and the human slave trade, as well as by gambling casinos, prostitution rings, financial hacking, blackmail, and murder.

> **If civilization is to embark upon a Renaissance of economic fairness, participative democracy, redeemable natural resources, and global peace, we must hope that knowledge about a path out of the cage of shame and oppression is spread as far and as wide as possible.**

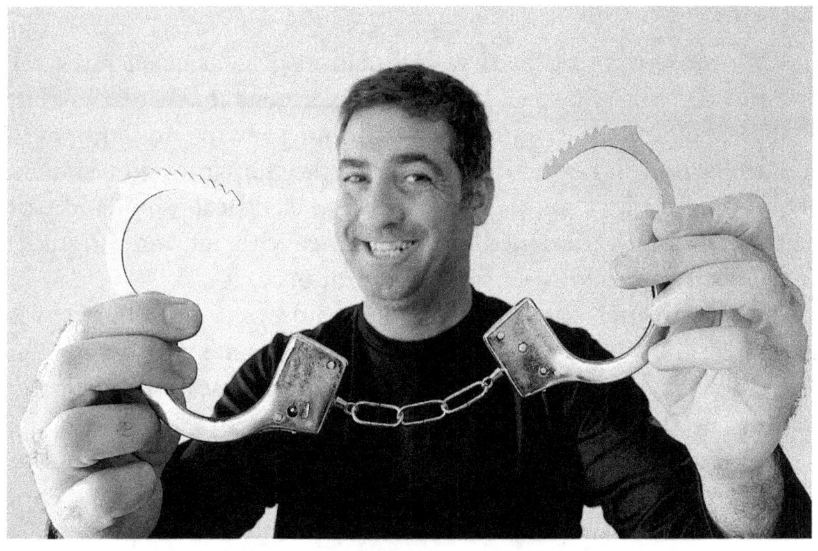

*

Theoretically, charged with a drive to approach and engage others in a loving manner, people who were once divided could peacefully unite.

It could start with small groups of neurologically healthy, bonded individuals. Some would emerge as multiple points of creative

49

leadership. As more and more divisive barriers are crossed, cells spread out like spokes from a multi-focal hub.

At some point, a mass coalition comprised of disparate social elements could galvanize. Perhaps this would appear that a *cult* grows into a **grassroots movement**, and then social plurality gains a **GRASSFIRE MOMENTUM…**

Imagine enlisting most of our population in non-violent resistance of the ruling elite, self-guided by acquired immunity from corporate systems of control or influence. Imagine how the corporate elite and the new rulers of our planet might be shocked. They would be impotent against a populist resistance movement, armed *only* with nearly unimaginable peaceful weapons of the psyche.

*

One more thing: Electrical stimulation of cells accelerates cellular division and growth. Could it also, then, accelerate cellular evolution?

The pea-sized prefrontal lobes continue growing until the mid-20's, and are poised to be the logical part of the human brain to champion evolution. In older persons, low-voltage electrical stimulation of the prefrontal lobes, designed to re-balance the left and right sides, dramatically improves cerebral organization.

The prefrontal cortex can then preside over and stabilize lower brain centers, such as the ancient reptilian brain's aggressive rage, or the crucial mid-brain limbic system, which is severely disrupted in trauma or PTSD.

The ultimate effect of accelerating cerebral evolution, or synchronizing brain function, might just mean that we as a species could shift to a plane beyond reptilian-driven war or exploitation.

Perhaps *then*, peace shall reign on Earth.

*

Technology for Social Reform

The red-bandana days are gone,
Never to come again;
And the days of freedom, force and fire,
Have dawned for this race of men…
…Peace to the ashes of the dead;
Success to the brave and new;
Tears for the dying race be shed.
Cheers for the bold and true!

"From the Desert," John Wesley Holloway, Neale Publishing Company: 1919, page 14
John Wesley Holloway is my great-grandfather.

Part Five: Summary and Call to Action

*

Evolutionary Activism

The emerging reality is that in some areas around the world, protest is becoming highly contested. Governments and police forces are losing their tolerance and targeting activists more and more. Moreover, many persons are either unable or reluctant to attend protest rallies, especially given the increasing criminalization of activists and protestors.

Non-violent action or civil resistance has succeeded as the middle road between passive acceptance of oppression and armed struggle against it. We all recall the honorable history of Mahatma Gandhi's resistance to the British occupation of India, Martin Luther King's brave struggle against segregation, and César Chávez's campaigns to protest the treatment of farm workers in California.

The wiser goal is to persuade people to change their behavior directly, rather than to persuade governments to change or not to change laws.

The altruistic, approach and engagement element of prefrontal balancing is essential to create a mass resistance movement. Only the right prefrontal qualities can confer the power and stamina to engage powerful activist strategies.

This is especially true when the adversary is an anonymous, global corporate elite that has effectively purchased our government, judiciary, military, and central bank. Even lobbying and political campaigning are at risky odds versus the increasing concentration of wealth in the hands of the very few. Relying on the electorate's participation in the democratic process—despite gerrymandering, aggressive corporate lobbying, and conservative financial contributions— is probably untenable and unsustainable long-term.

53

Technology for Social Reform

Only by first desensitizing the populace to shame, and then re-evoking the human love response, can social progress maintain its current momentum.

*

Let's correlate the methodology of activism for social change with the biotechnological advantages of anti-oppression training. The advantages of therapy for all activist strategies should be obvious.

<table><tr><td>

<u>Results of anti-oppression training:</u>
- Euphoria, energy, and adaptability…
- Precognition, telepathy, clairvoyance…
- Creativity, originality, inventiveness, ingenuity…
- Curiosity, openness, and absence of judgmental prejudice…
- Empathy, altruism, and drive to approach and engage other people…
- Autonomy and motivation to acquire rights and satisfy needs without postponement…

</td></tr></table>

Please pause, and consider how the above qualities might be helpful for yourself as an advocate for social change, especially when applied to non-violent protest strategies:

<table><tr><td>

<u>Methods of non-violent resistance:</u>
- Community building— especially in the sense of cooperative or grassroots movements…
- Lobbying and political campaigning…
- Civil disobedience and economic activism—especially by boycotting unethical corporations, and purchasing from independent retailers instead…
- Organizing rallies—for fundraising, but especially to persuade others to make phone calls, send text messages, share social media posts, vote, and "talk" …

</td></tr></table>

An impressive article, *Inspired Voices: 5 Unconventional forms of Activism, Elephant Journal (April 24, 2015),* which is based on the book: *Beautiful Trouble: A Tool Box for Revolution, by Andrew Boyd and Dave Oswald Mitchell,* conveys enchanting messages about the plausible future of social activism.

About altruism:

The point is to show that not only are there alternatives to not standing up for what you believe, but there are great alternatives that bring communities back together, caring for all instead of the few.

About anti-oppression training:

One view holds that acknowledging privileges and oppressions on a daily basis ranks as a form of activism."

About love, self-love, and toxic shame:

If we do not help ourselves, it is not likely that we have a ton of left over energy to help others. In the words of Audre Lorde, 'Caring for myself is not self-indulgence, it is self-preservation, and that is an act of political warfare'...

In a society that teaches us that we are not *good* enough, not thin enough, *pretty* enough, *manly* enough, *feminine* enough or *smart* enough, not allowing ourselves to buy into that and knowing that we are good enough is one the biggest ways to say **"F-you"** to the system.

Love yourself, and love others. By shedding light on our own tiny corners of the universe we are changing the world, even if it's only by a fraction.

CALL TO ACTION

I am convinced that just learning about the mere existence of shame, and being able to recognize it in oneself and others, will dramatically alter our collective future. To go further, and realize that all persons, aside from the ultra-wealthy, are being subjected to escalating abuse that verges on neoslavery, will dismantle divisiveness over minor issues and liberal-conservative polarization in our society.

To begin to employ *any* anti-oppression or shame desensitization processes will be a definitive advantage for all non-violent social activists in their effort to create a sustainable resistance movement against the corporate elite.

I do not expect or wish for all human beings to undergo a massive neurological treatment, unless they so choose for a variety of possible reasons. But I *do* hope that emerging, new social engineers and activists will learn about the neuro-technologies that I am utilizing—for ignorance may permit the same technologies to continue to be developed and used *against* us.

Currently, training using trans-cranial electrical stimulation is required of virtually all active duty soldiers in the Middle East, presumably to increase visual-motor coordination when firing in combat. Yet, the ripple effects may be to increase the soldier's subordination to authority, decrease his or her compassion for the victims of violence, and increase a false alarm rate—perhaps firing when no threat exists, such as at unarmed bystanders or children (Pavlidou et al., 2012).

What I ask of you and your organization:

- Please pass this pamphlet on to your colleagues and followers.

- Encourage open debate and discussion about this treatise and material.

- Invite those who wish to know more to read **"Overcoming Oppression"**—If they do not have the money to buy either the Kindle version or the paperback book on Amazon, they can contact me through my website and I will email them a PDF version to print and/or forward to others.

- Consider inviting me to public presentations, talk to groups, or do trainings, as a personal connection with me will vastly help the learning curve for most listeners.

- Introduce my work to your connections, followers or subscribers via email and social media lists, and post essays that I will gladly write for your blogs or websites—but *only* as you deem appropriate, ethical, and helpful.

- Connect with me personally for questions or further assistance, as well as to keep up-to-date with the evolution of the "Paradigm-shifting and Brain-freeing Project."

I look forward to working with you, and with progressive nonprofit organizations that you may belong to. If you read my books or social media posts, you will understand my lifelong involvement with social change, my passionate commitment to leave a positive legacy for future generations, and my honesty and transparency.

Michael Holloway King, MD

MICHAEL H. KING, MD

mkingpsi7149@yahoo.com
(760) 894-8208

Website and blog: www.michaelhollowayking.com
I prefer to receive non-urgent contact via my website.

https://www.amazon.com/author/michaelhollowayking
http://www.linkedin.com/pub/michael-king-m-d/36/442/370
https://www.you.tube.com/channel/UCEeS-qDgtKqfFLAiWX9-VcA
www.facebook.com/michaelhollowayking/
www.facebook.com/michaelhollowayking2/

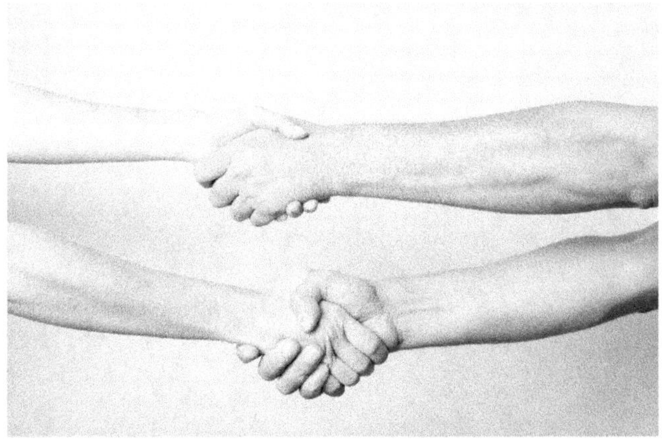

59

BIOSKETCH: MICHAEL HOLLOWAY KING, MD

Michael King, MD is a graduate from both Harvard College and Harvard Medical School and he has had over four decades of experience in healthcare and communication skills. His love for biopersonality, consciousness, neuropsychiatry and international health prepared him to explore the essence of human nature.

Although he specialized in mind-body therapy in his alternative practice, he has *also* worked in virtually all aspects of conventional medicine. He is currently a pioneer in social engineering and the first physician to address shame and social oppression, pinpoint their psychobiological roots, and invent treatment programs to resist them.

Dr. King is an expert in writing technology, listening skills, and public speaking, so writing a multi-genre, memoir-driven novel, "Hide and Play Dead," came as naturally as his self-help professional literature in "Overcoming Oppression."

Michael currently has a private practice in psychotherapy and psychiatry near Palm Springs, California where he specializes in the treatment of shame, abuse, trauma, and social oppression. His treatment process is based on high empathy, high rapport, client-centered approaches, along with somatic therapy and non-invasive emerging technologies in the neurosciences.

His current writing projects are a study manual and workbook to accompany "Overcoming Oppression," and a guide to his treatment system for healthcare professionals. Many experts believe that his work may represent a paradigm shift for most of the social and political sciences, economics, and, especially, the field of medicine.

It is time for the healer to emerge from behind the walls of clinical medicine, and tackle the social milieu where illness is perpetuated.

It is time for a new and revolutionary branch of medicine to take a stand against the primary source of human suffering in the world today—social oppression.

Technology for Social Reform